OCD TREATMENT MANUAL FOR CHILDREN

A OBSESSIVE COMPULSIVE DISORDER TREATMENT MANUAL FOR CBT THERAPISTS, CBT THERAPISTS IN TRAINING & TRAINEE CLINICAL PSYCHOLOGISTS: THIS OCD BOOK EXPLAINS THE MEANING OF OCD AND INCLUDES AN EXPLANATION OF OCD DISORDER, OCD TESTS, OCD LISTS, AND SIGNS OF OCD SYMPTOMS

Written Dr Nicola Ridgeway & Dr James Manning

Illustrations by Francesca Apichella

CBT Worksheets for Kids Aged 8 to 13 - OCD.

The Authors

Dr Nicola Ridgeway is a Consultant Clinical Psychologist and an accredited cognitive and behavioural therapist. She lectured on Cognitive Behaviour Therapy (CBT) at the University of East Anglia, Norfolk, England, and the University of Essex for many years before becoming the Clinical Director of the West Suffolk CBT Service Ltd. Together with Dr James Manning she has co-authored several books on CBT.

Dr James Manning is a Consultant Clinical Psychologist and the Managing Director of the West Suffolk CBT Service. James has post-graduate qualifications in both Clinical Psychology and Counselling Psychology. He has regularly offered workshops and training to clinicians throughout the United Kingdom on CBT and continues to work as a therapist.

By the authors

How to Help Your Loved One Overcome Depression

The Little Book on CBT for Depression

CBT Worksheets

My CBT Journal

CBT Worksheets for Anxiety

CBT Worksheets for Depression

CBT Worksheets for Panic Attacks

CBT Worksheets for Teenage Social Anxiety

Fused: A memoire of childhood OCD and adult obsession

Contents

How to use this book

This book has been written for trainee CBT therapists and clinical psychologists in training. It has been designed specifically for clinicians who are working with children and adolescents with obsessive compulsive distress and obsessive compulsive disorder (OCD). The worksheets, handouts and templates will also be useful to experienced clinicians who would like to streamline their work with clients.

If you are reading a hardcopy of this book, you are welcome to photocopy its contents. This book has been set out with broad margins to make pages easy to copy. Alternatively, if this book is a PDF copy purchased from **www.PDF-Books.com**, you are welcome to print out as many copies as you would like for your clinical work.

This book has six sections:

Section 1 focuses on assessing OCD. The questionnaires have been designed to be child-friendly, non-threatening and to draw out information to enhance initial **formulations** (psychological explanations of presenting problems). In order to use the assessments in Section 1 effectively, clients will need to have already read the booklet 'Joe goes to OCD school' (located in Section 6 of this book).

Section 2 contains useful templates to assist clinicians to collect information about thoughts and feelings.

This information can then be used in **Section 3**, where general CBT maintenance cycles as well as specific OCD maintenance cycles are introduced.

Section 4 demonstrates how generic CBT cycles can be used for intervention, and includes templates designed to: a) draw out core beliefs; b) create balanced thoughts, and c) place new information in positive generic CBT cycles.

Section 5 has a collection of worksheets that can be used for intervention. These worksheets can be used in sessions and/or given out as homework after they have been utilised in sessions.

Section 6 includes a selection of handouts that can be offered to clients before or after sessions. The handout 'Joe goes to OCD school' gives a thorough overview of OCD and what might be expected in therapy. Additional handouts explain: a) how to work with OCD urges; b) how to form a positive relationship with feelings, and c) how brain architecture works.

Assessing OCD

Many children who have OCD may have suffered unnecessarily for years. Due to this, it is imperative to carry out a thorough assessment. Assessment will generally need to be completed with both the child and their parent or carer present, or important information is likely to be overlooked. Ideally, prior to assessment your client will have read the handout/booklet at the back of this book called 'Joe goes to OCD school'. This handout is designed to: a) offer psycho-education about OCD; b) assist children to recognise that everyone's OCD is different and that it affects people in different ways, and c) encourage disclosure, as shame and fear connected with OCD often act as a barrier to openness.

This section includes child-friendly worksheets that can be used to draw out important information in a non-threatening way. Worksheets have been designed to harness both 'externalising' and 'third person' approaches. These worksheets can be used to help clients: a) make a list of their OCD neutralising behaviours; b) identify intrusive thoughts; c) externalise their OCD, and d) track the impact of their OCD over the course of a week.

Benefits of this section:

- Brings client's awareness to the scale of the problems experienced.
- Helps to develop a problem list.
- Draws out intrusive thought content in a non-threatening way.
- Assists in the development of the therapist's initial formulation.
- Useful for homework exercises.
- Can assist in the development of collaboration between therapist and client.
- Encourages the development of goal-based behaviour.
- Draws out information that can be useful in setting agendas.

Identifying neutralising behaviours: questionnaire

This questionnaire is designed to assist child clients to identify their neutralising behaviours by comparing themselves to Joe, the main character in 'Joe goes to OCD school' (see Section 6, page 85). The questionnaire covers 11 of the most common neutralising behaviour themes that are carried out by children with OCD. It can often be beneficial to complete this questionnaire with your client, offering further examples of behaviours that may be more specific to your client's difficulties. This will help to draw out additional information. If answering some of these questions feels too threatening to your client, it can help to switch to a third person questioning approach, for example, asking: 'Are there any other behaviours that you think Joe might carry out that are not on this list?'

Summary of benefits:

- Identifies neutralising behaviours.
- Non-judgemental assessment instrument.

Do you have any behaviours that are similar to Joe's?

Look through the behaviours that Joe has below. Tick ✔ the boxes where you may do the same thing or something similar.

1. Doing the same things over and over again. For example, tapping objects, washing hands.

☐

2. Checking that things are locked or turned off over and over again.

☐

3. Placing objects in a particular order or grouping objects.

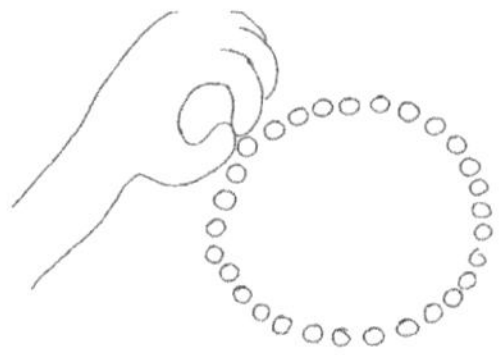

☐

4. Doing things in a particular order and becoming very upset if anyone changes the order or interrupts the order.

☐

Do you have any behaviours that are similar to Joe's? (Cont.)

Look through the behaviours that Joe has below. Tick ✔ the boxes where you may do the same thing or something similar.

5. Repeatedly counting and recounting.

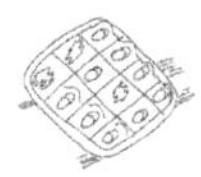

☐

6. Asking the same questions over and over again.

☐

7. Needing things to be placed in a particular way.

☐

8. Going back to places you have already been to and doing things in the same order.

☐

Do you have any behaviours that are similar to Joe's? (Cont.)

Look through the behaviours that Joe has below. Tick ✓ the boxes where you may do the same thing or something similar.

9. Repeatedly asking for reassurance.

☐

10. Saying words over and over in my head, or continuously repeating sounds in my head.

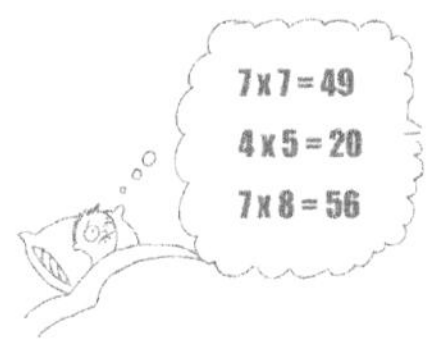

☐

11. Avoiding certain objects, places or people.

☐

12. Do you have any different behaviours to Joe? Write what you do in the box.

Making a list

One of the most important tasks to complete after identifying general areas of neutralisation (see previous worksheet) is to make a detailed list of all the neutralising behaviours that your client engages in. These behaviours may be: a) observable actions that the client carries out by him/herself, for example, checking rituals; b) actions that involve others, for example, requesting reassurance, or c) internal cognitive neutralisers, such as counting or completing the times tables. Parents who accompany their child to an assessment will usually come prepared with several examples of neutralising behaviours.

If a list is not completed during the assessment meeting, it can be set as a homework task instead. In their day-to-day lives, children and parents will often notice neutralising behaviours that they forgot to mention in their assessment appointment and will bring them to your attention in later sessions.

With completed lists in front of them, your clients are likely to become aware of just how entrenched their OCD neutralisers have become. This list will also be useful for setting agendas in future therapy sessions, and for continuously reviewing progress.

Benefits of making a list:

- Increases client awareness of the scale of the problems experienced.
- Doubles as a problem list.
- Works as a helpful homework exercise.
- Operates as a beneficial review instrument that encourages goal-based behaviour.
- Assists in setting agendas.

Making a List

Use the list below to make a note of everything that your OCD makes you do. Put as many things on your list as possible. Ask your parents or care givers for ideas as sometimes they may be able to spot things that you do not notice.

Things my OCD makes me do

1. Shower after I have been outside.
2. Make sure people take their shoes off when they come in.
3. Put clothes in washing basket if they have been outside.
4. Vacuum bedroom if anyone else has been in it.
5. Avoid areas of the house that are contaminated.
6. Clean my body when I shower in the same order.
7. Complete night-time routine in the same order.
8. Bed sheets need to be exactly straight before I get into bed.
9. Mum needs to answer my questions using exactly the same words every time.
10. The night light needs to be switched on.

Making a List

Use the list below to make a note of everything that your OCD makes you do. Put as many things on your list as possible. Ask your parents or care givers for ideas as sometimes they may be able to spot things that you do not notice.

Things my OCD makes me do

1.

2.

3.

4.

5.

6.

7.

8.

9.

10.

Identifying intrusive thoughts

Many children find it difficult to openly state the content of their intrusive thoughts during assessment. This can be for a variety of reasons. For example, it could be the case that they: a) cannot recall the content of their intrusive thoughts, or b) do not want to reveal their intrusive thoughts for fear that by talking about them the thoughts may somehow become real or happen. In CBT this process is referred to as **thought action fusion**. Thought action fusion, as the words suggest, leads OCD sufferers to believe that they can make bad things happen or stop bad things from happening just by thinking about it.

This questionnaire* is designed to help children notice their intrusive thoughts. Later in therapy, when the child has been socialised to the CBT model, the therapist can return to the completed questionnaire and ask open questions to draw out the full content of intrusive thoughts.

*This questionnaire uses the word 'worries' rather than the words 'intrusive thoughts' to make the concept more accessible to children.

Benefits of using a questionnaire to identify intrusive thoughts:

- Draws out intrusive thought content in a non-threatening way.
- Assists in the development of the therapist's initial CBT formulation.
- Helps clients to feel understood.

Do you have any worries that are similar to Joe's?

Look through the worries that Joe has below. Tick ✔ the boxes where you may worry about the same thing or something similar.

1. Thinking about germs or being sick.

☐

2. Worrying about friends or family members being hurt.

☐

3. Worries about not being safe.

☐

4. Worries about being seriously ill.

☐

Do you have any worries that are similar to Joe's?

Look through the worries that Joe has below. Tick ✓ the boxes where you may worry about the same thing or something similar.

5. Worries about upsetting others.

☐

6. Fears about things being uneven.

☐

7. Worries about making a mistake.

☐

8. Worries about things being unlucky.

☐

Do you have any worries that are similar to Joe's? (Cont.)

Look through the worries that Joe has below. Tick ✓ the boxes where you may worry about the same thing or something similar.

9. Thoughts about hurting others even though you would never do it.

☐

10. Thoughts about losing control and suddenly breaking the rules.

☐

11. Do you have any worries that are different to Joe's? If you do, write them in the box below.

Drawing an OCD monster

Externalising principles are commonly used by most CBT programmes for OCD. Externalising OCD may involve children giving their OCD a name, thinking of what their OCD might look like, or viewing their OCD as a separate personality.

This book sets out to externalise OCD as a somewhat misguided monster. A monster that unwittingly grows out of control, causing chaos for the individual, while failing in its intention to be protective and helpful. Viewing their OCD as a monster offers children a construct whereby they can view their OCD as an entity that can be managed, trained and made smaller by using a variety of CBT strategies.

A useful way to introduce an externalising approach is to ask your child client to draw what their OCD looks like. Drawing their OCD monsters will help children to cement OCD as a construct in their minds.

Summary of uses:

- Can be used as a homework exercise.
- Can assist in the development of trust between therapist and client. This occurs as therapist and client think together about how they can reduce the power of the OCD monster.
- Separates OCD from who the client is as a person.

If you had an OCD monster what would it look like?

Draw your OCD monster in the box and give it a name.

My OCD monster is called ______________________________

How big is your OCD?

Based on externalising principles, these worksheets can be used by your clients to track how powerful they feel their OCD has been over the course of a week. If fluctuations are noticed, this can lead to a discussion between the therapist and client. Open questions asked by the therapist can draw out triggering events, environmental factors, or other issues that may be exacerbating anxiety leading to associated neutralising behaviour.

Summary of uses:

- Can be used to track the impact of OCD over time.
- Develops an externalising approach towards OCD.
- Can be used to identify triggers for OCD.

How big is your OCD?

Use this chart to draw how big your OCD is for each day of the week.

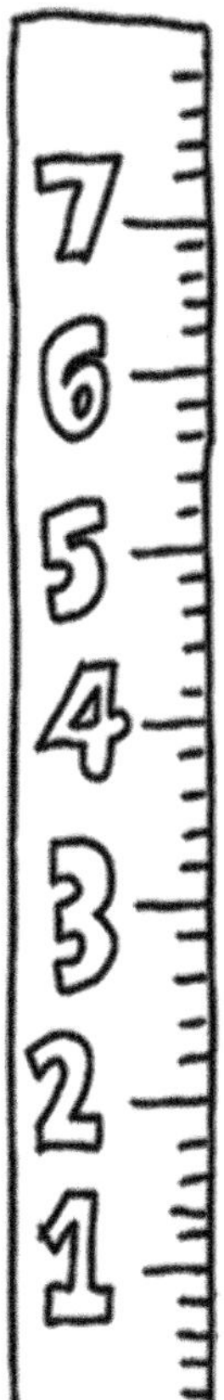

MONDAY **TUESDAY** **WEDNESDAY** **THURSDAY**

How big is your OCD?

Use this chart to draw how big your OCD is for each day of the week.

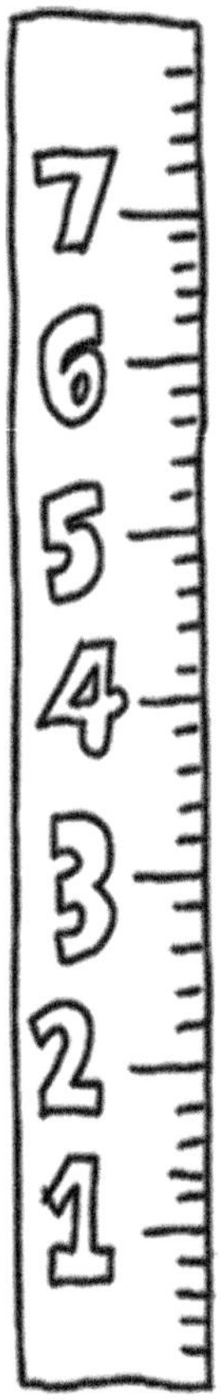

FRIDAY SATURDAY SUNDAY

Section 2

Identifying thoughts and feelings

This section is designed to assist clients to identify their negative and frightening thoughts. After thoughts have been recorded clients can then start to make connections between thoughts and feelings.

Using the worksheets in this section will help clients to step back and take more of an observational stance towards thoughts and feelings.

Benefits of this section:

- Helps to identify thoughts.
- Can be used for homework exercises.
- Encourages detachment from thoughts.

Identifying frightening thoughts

Frightening/intrusive thoughts and negative automatic thoughts form an essential component of CBT maintenance models and, as such, it is important to identify them. The following two thoughts sheets can be used by your clients to write down the type of thoughts that affect them. Writing down thoughts utilises central executive processes, puts emotional distance between your clients and their thoughts, and can encourage reflective processes.

Summary of uses:

- Helps to identify thoughts.
- Can be used as a homework exercise.
- Encourages detachment from thoughts.

MY FRIGHTENING THOUGHTS

Mum and Dad being in a car accident.
Dying of a heart attack.
Burglars breaking into the house.
My friends being hurt.
I have cancer.
I'm going to be sick.
I've got germs on me.
My teacher shouting at me.

MY FRIGHTENING THOUGHTS

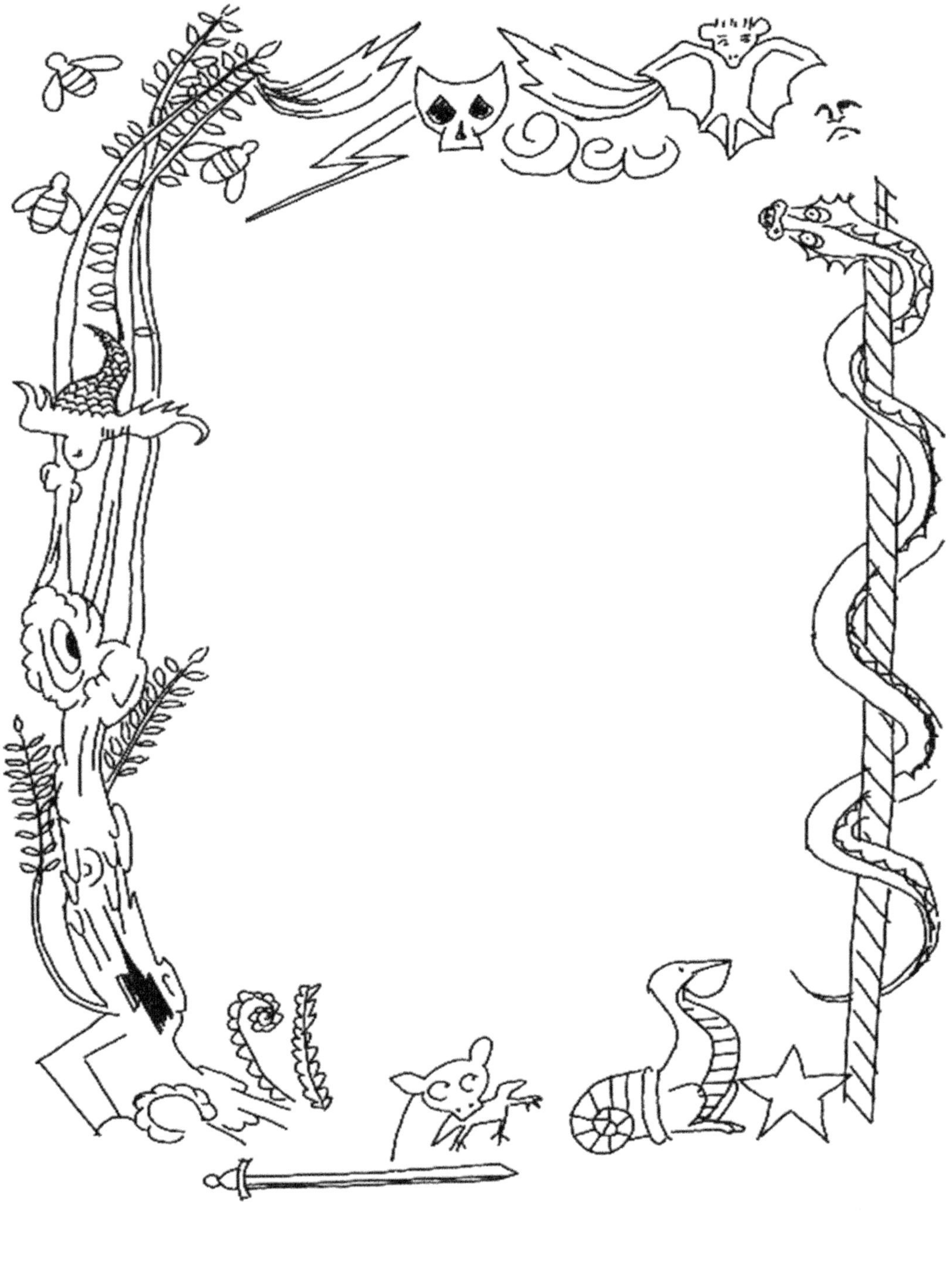

MY NEGATIVE THOUGHTS

People treat me unfairly.

Mum doesn't trust me.

The coach always subs me for no reason.

I get the blame for everything.

I hate myself.

Mum loves my sister more than me.

My teacher gives me bad marks because she doesn't like me.

MY NEGATIVE THOUGHTS

Making connections between thoughts and feelings

In early stages of CBT for OCD, children can be encouraged to make connections between their thoughts and their feelings. Thoughts and feelings can often pass through awareness in such a transient way that many children may not recognise that the types of thoughts they have directly impact on the way that they feel.

Encouraging children to write down their thoughts and feelings on one sheet assists them to step back and observe how they feel as they hold a thought in mind. This process might sound simplistic; however, it is a very useful and fundamental experiential process that socialises children to the CBT model of emotional disorder.

Summary of uses:

- Helps to connect thoughts and feelings.
- Socialises children to the CBT model.
- Can be used as a homework exercise.

HOW DO DIFFERENT THOUGHTS AFFECT THE WAY WE FEEL?

Guess what Joe is thinking about. Draw a line between how Joe is feeling and his thought.

CATCHING YOUR THOUGHTS AND NOTICING HOW THEY MAKE YOU FEEL

Use this table to write down your thoughts. Write the number that is closest to how you feel.

My thought, for example, 'I think I might be sick'.	**1 2 3 4 5 6** 
I might have done my homework wrong. My teacher might tell me off.	1
I touched my bag, and it was on the floor.	3
Mum and Dad should be back by now.	5

CATCHING YOUR THOUGHTS AND NOTICING HOW THEY MAKE YOU FEEL

Use this table to write down your thoughts. Draw a face that shows how you feel.

My thought, for example, 'I think I might be sick'.	

Drawing out CBT cycles

Placing thoughts, feelings and behaviours into cycles can offer an understandable way for clients to view their problems. This section has worksheets designed to draw out simple CBT cycles, specific OCD cycles and more complex OCD cycles. The cycle selected for use with clients can be determined by the client's developmental level and/or cognitive ability.

Benefits of this section:

- Increases awareness of how problems are being maintained.
- Assists in the development of the therapist's initial formulation.
- Useful for homework exercises.
- Can assist in the development of collaboration between therapist and client.
- Encourages the development of goal-based behaviour.
- Draws out information that can be useful in setting agendas.

Placing thoughts, feelings and behaviours into cycles

Thought, feelings and behaviour cycles are the simplest type of psychological formulation within CBT. Arrows are generally drawn between each of the three components (thoughts, feelings and behaviours) to demonstrate: a) the interconnectedness between components and b) how components reinforce one another.

Before cycles are created, thoughts, feelings and behaviour diaries are generally utilised to collect the necessary information. Diaries should always be completed in sessions with clients before they are given out as homework.

Once clients become familiar with CBT cycles, clients can gain a greater understanding about how their thoughts and feelings can result in neutralising behaviours.

Summary of uses:

- Useful for creating simple formulations.
- Socialises clients to the cognitive model.
- Helps clients to engage in a process of observation.
- Can be used as a homework exercise.

PUTTING THOUGHTS, FEELINGS AND BEHAVIOURS INTO CYCLES

HOW DO THOUGHTS AND FEELINGS AFFECT WHAT I DO?

Use this table to write down your thoughts and feelings and what you did.

My thought, for example, 'I think I might be sick'.	Feeling, e.g., 	What I did, for example, washed my hands.
I think I've done my homework wrong. The teacher is going to tell me off.	Anxious, sweating.	Did the homework again just in case. Handed it in to the teacher.
Mum and Dad have been in an accident.	Frightened, anxious.	Kept looking out the window to check if they were coming. Phoned Mum.
What if my heart stops beating?	Anxious, heart beating fast.	Asked my Aunty if I was going to die.

HOW DO THOUGHTS AND FEELINGS AFFECT WHAT I DO?

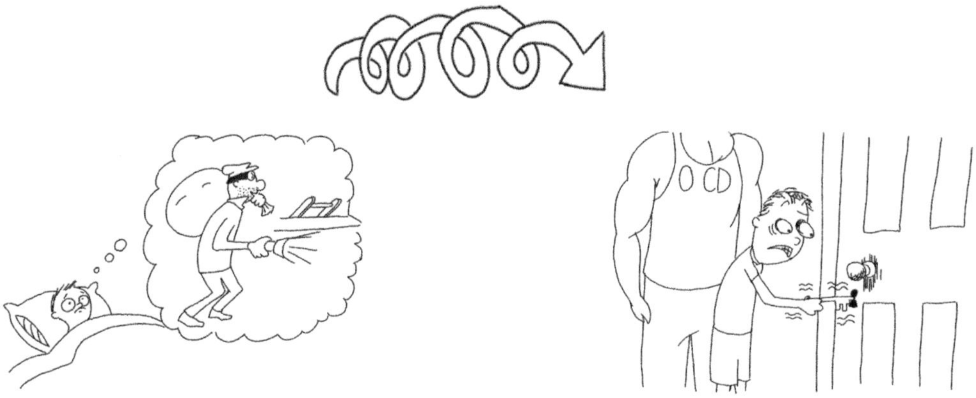

Use this table to write down your thoughts and feelings and what you did.

My thought, for example, 'I think I might be sick'.	Feeling, e.g., 	What I did, for example, washed my hands.

THOUGHTS, FEELINGS AND BEHAVIOUR CYCLES

Draw or write your information on this sheet to make your own cycle.

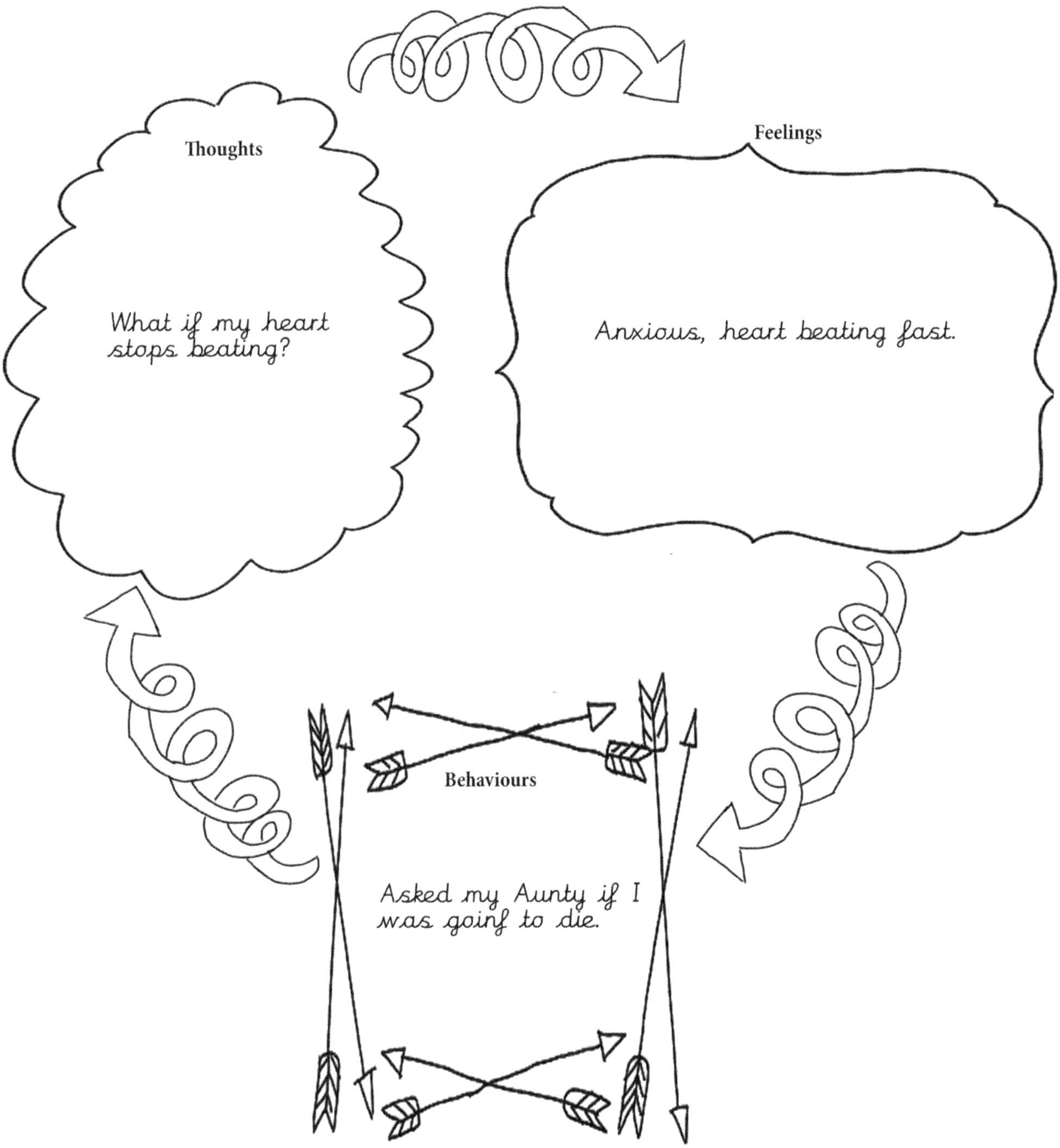

THOUGHTS, FEELINGS AND BEHAVIOUR CYCLES

Draw or write your information on this sheet to make your own cycle.

Thoughts, feelings and behaviour cycles: the generic OCD model

The generic CBT model for OCD includes sections for: a) trigger situations; b) intrusive thoughts; c) emotions, and d) neutralising behaviours.

The trigger could be something in: a) the child's internal environment (e.g., becoming aware of an ectopic heart beat); or b) the child's external environment (e.g., seeing a shop worker touch bread with his/her hands without wearing gloves).

Summary of uses:

- Useful for creating simple OCD formulations.
- Socialises child clients to the cognitive model.
- Helps clients to engage in observation processes.
- Can be used as a homework exercise.

THOUGHT, FEELING AND BEHAVIOUR CYCLES FOR OCD

Trigger situation

Notice the car is not in the driveway.

Intrusive thoughts

A thought about Mum and Dad being in a car accident.

Emotions and feelings in body

Feel really upset. Anxious feeling in tummy and chest.

NeutralIsing behaviour

Try to contact Mum to make sure that she is OK.

THOUGHT, FEELING AND BEHAVIOUR CYCLES FOR OCD

More complex OCD models

More complex CBT models add avoidant behaviours to psychological formulations for OCD. The model shown on the next page begins with a trigger situation that in turn activates an intrusive thought (see Rachman, Coughtrey, & Radomsky, 2015*). The intrusive thought produces a feeling, usually anxiety and/or guilt, which is activated by the meaning of the intrusive thought. To reduce distress, the individual carries out neutralising and/or avoidant behaviour. This behaviour reinforces the fear of the trigger situation.

An example could be Joe finding himself sitting near to his brother (the trigger). While sitting next to his brother, he has a thought about lashing out and hurting his brother (the intrusive thought). This leads Joe to feel anxious (the emotion). Joe's anxiety is driven by the thought that he is a dangerous person for having such a thought (the meaning). Joe tries not to sit near his brother (avoidance) and keeps his hands in his pockets if he has to sit near his brother (the neutraliser). Joe's behaviour reaffirms his fear of sitting close to his brother (the trigger).

Summary of uses:

- Explains how triggers are reinforced.
- Helps clients to understand that their behaviour is self-defeating at a logical level.

* Rachman, S., Coughtrey, S.R. & Radomsky, A. (2015) The Oxford Guide to the Treatment of Mental Contamination. The Oxford University Press.

HOW MY OCD GETS STRONGER

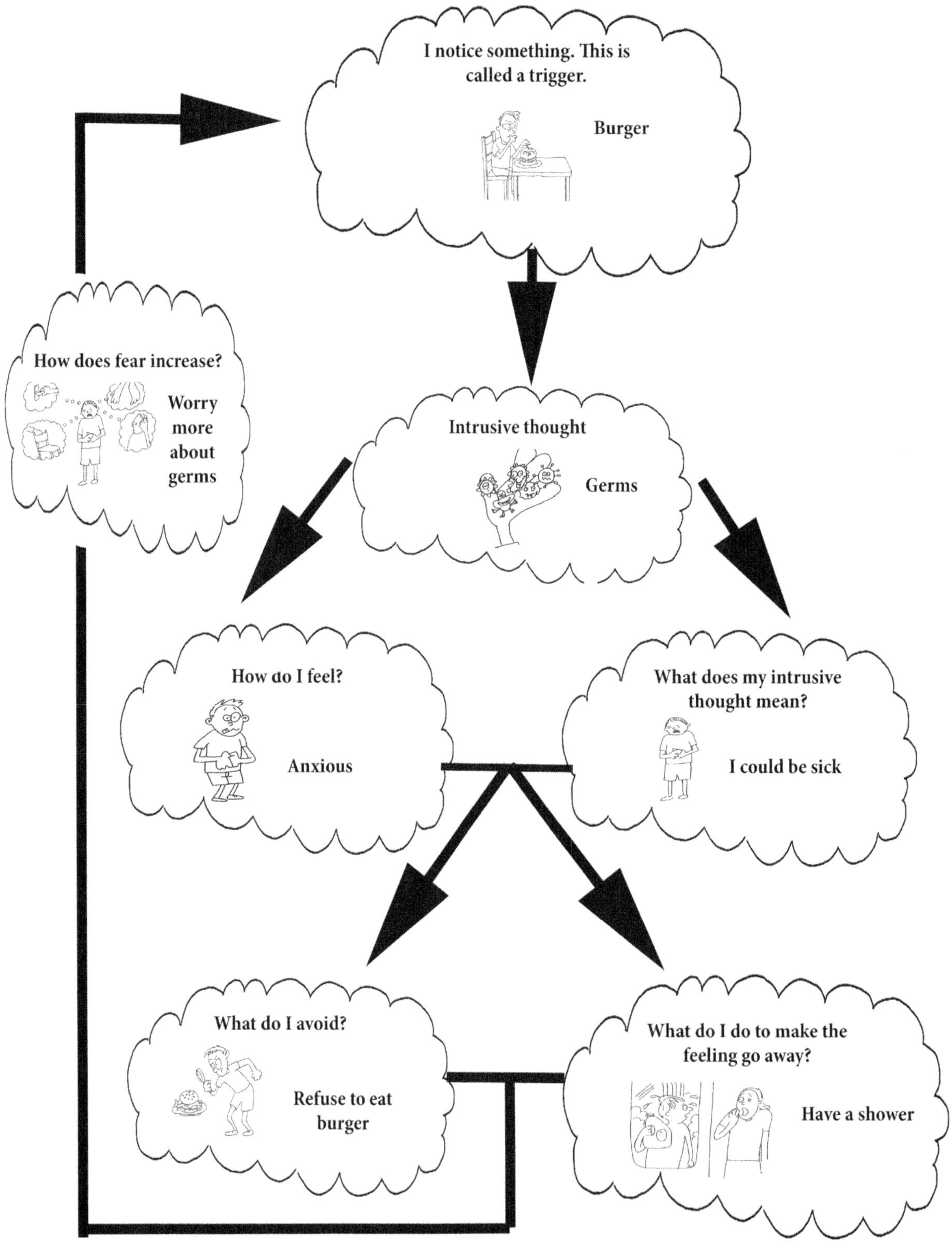

HOW MY OCD GETS STRONGER

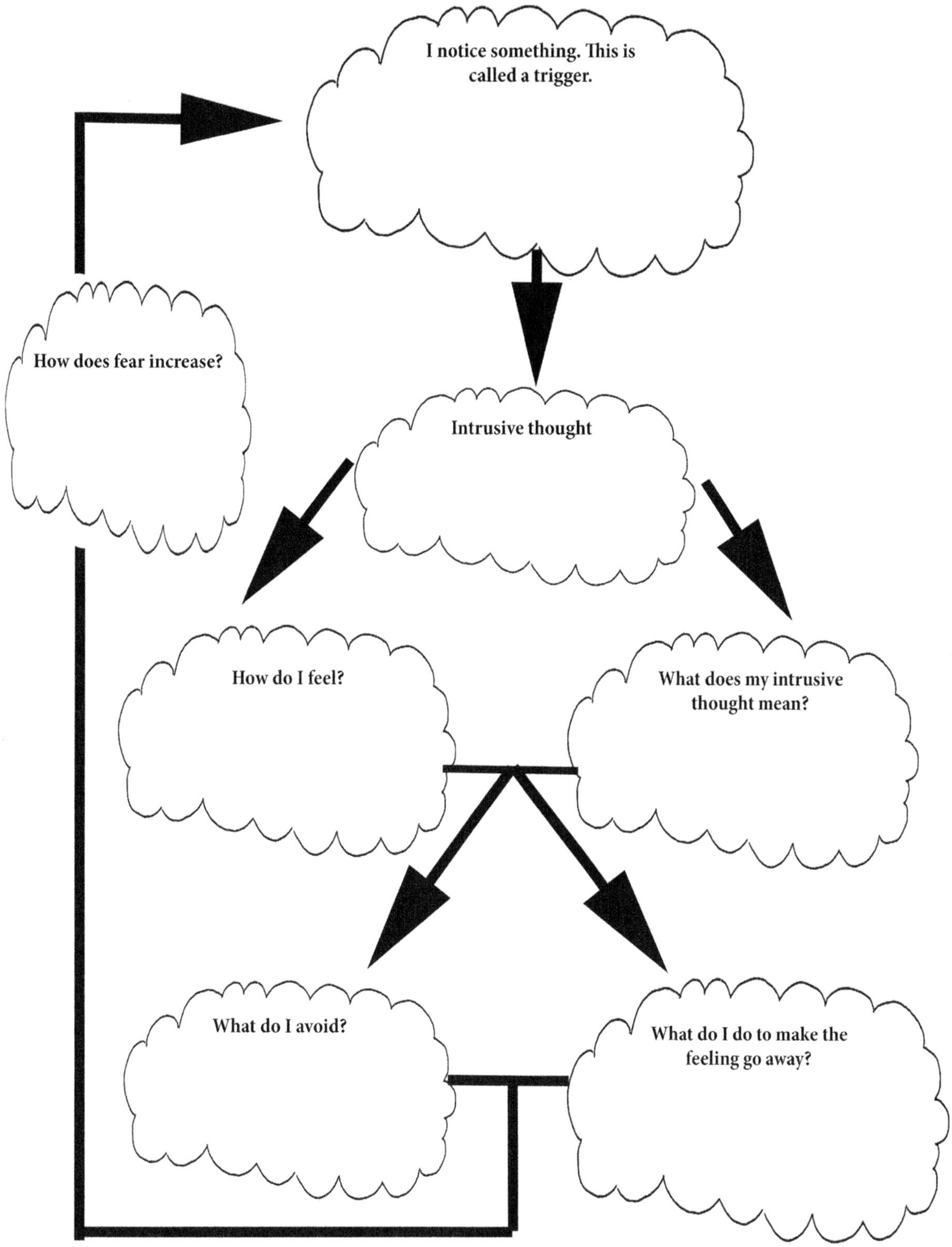

Using generic CBT cycles for intervention

Generic CBT cycles can be very effective instruments for showing clients their self-defeating behaviours and/or self-fulfilling prophecies. When this occurs, clients tend to become more motivated to break negative patterns. Included within generic CBT cycles are areas dedicated to: a) negative automatic thoughts or upsetting thoughts, and b) the meaning behind thoughts. Meanings behind thoughts can be uncovered by using a 'downward arrow' exercise. (In this book, the 'downward arrow' exercise is referred to as a 'deepest fear' exercise). Upsetting thoughts can be challenged by looking at evidence for and against the thoughts that lead to the creation of more balanced thoughts. Once more balanced thoughts have been generated they can be placed in new positive generic CBT cycles. Positive generic cycles can be incredibly useful as they act as a guide for new, alternative, more positive behaviours, which often leads to goal- or solution-based thinking.

Benefits of the worksheets in this section:

- Brings client's awareness to self-fulfilling prophecies.
- Helps to encourage solution-focused behaviour.
- Helps to access core beliefs.
- Clearly demonstrates self-defeating cycles.
- Excellent for socialising clients to the cognitive model.
- Can assist in the development of collaboration between therapist and client.
- Can be used to reduce distress associated with negative thoughts.
- Can be offered as homework.
- Guides future behaviour.

Deepest fear exercise

Essential to using generic CBT cycles for intervention is identifying the meaning behind negative automatic thoughts. Within adult CBT, beliefs are usually uncovered by using the 'downward arrow' exercise. Thoughts and feelings are continuously followed, with the therapist asking, 'If that were true, what would that say/mean about you?' Questioning continues until core beliefs are identified. The downward arrow approach can also be used with child clients. For the most part, children's core beliefs are easier to identify than adults, as children tend to have fewer defences in place, and they are less likely to engage in over-analytical thinking (as their neocortex is still developing and growing).

Once a belief is uncovered, emotional distress is likely to be triggered. Clients will need to be congratulated for having the courage to reveal their core beliefs, and psycho-education will need to be offered to the child about the nature of beliefs. (Ostensibly, beliefs are very strongly held ideas that cannot be proved right or wrong using evidence or facts.)

Summary of uses:

- Can be used to access core beliefs.

DEEPEST FEAR EXERCISE

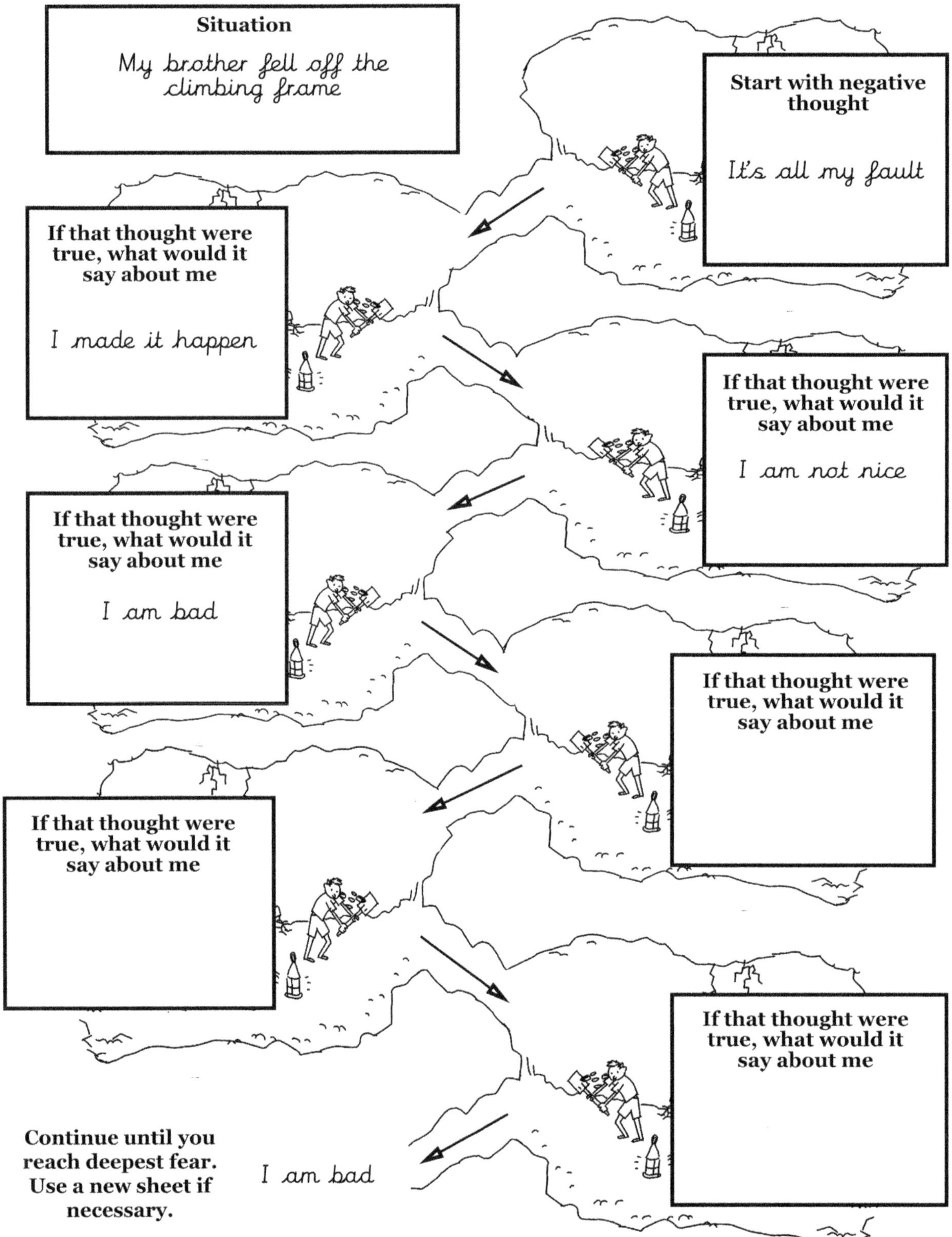

DEEPEST FEAR EXERCISE

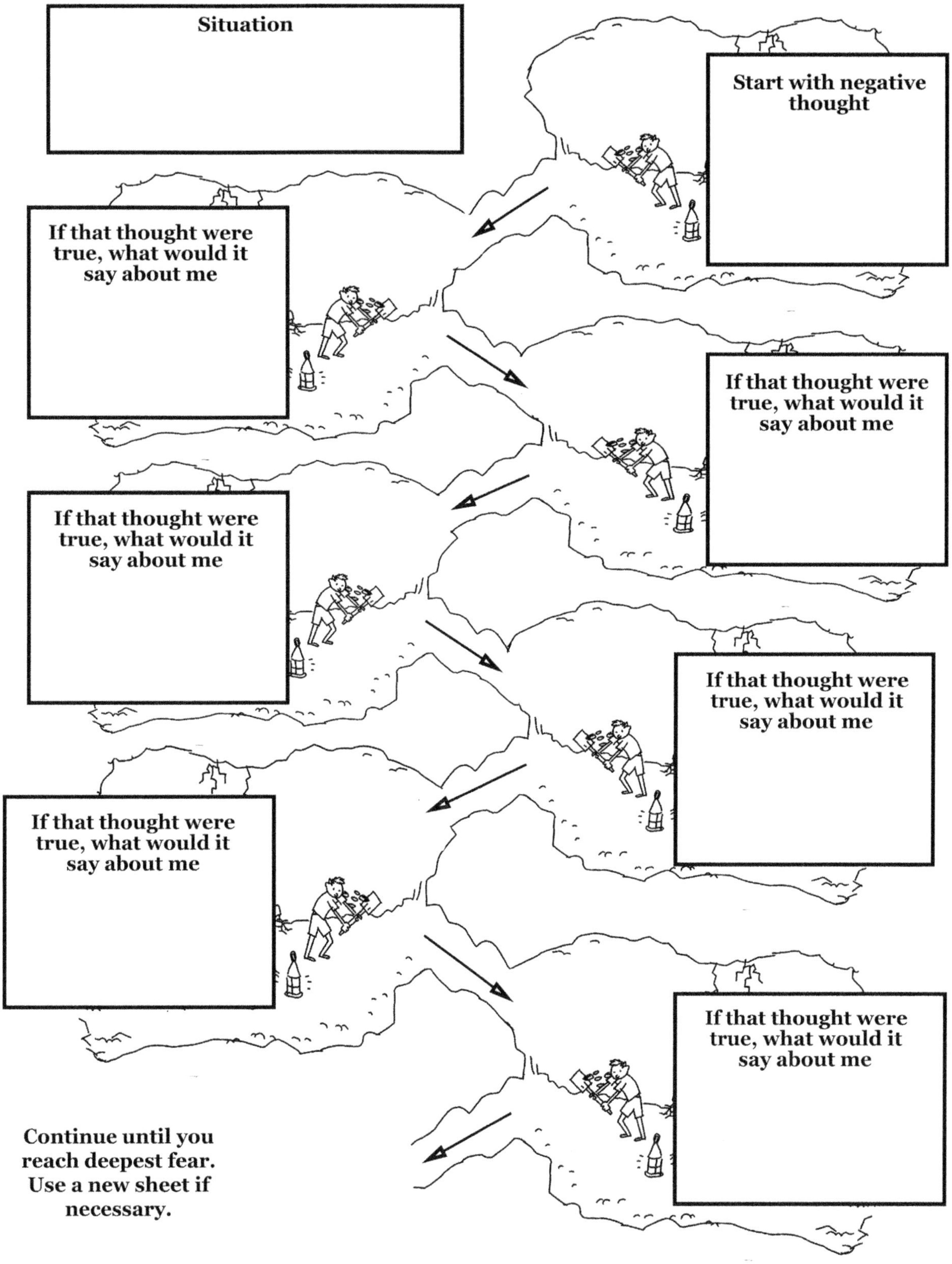

Continue until you reach deepest fear. Use a new sheet if necessary.

The generic CBT model

The generic CBT model can be used with children if the child's level of understanding permits its use. As with all other CBT models, it can also be used to formulate clients' problems for supervision or for case presentations. The generic CBT model is most commonly used to demonstrate a connection between beliefs, thoughts, feelings, physiology and behaviour. A particular benefit of the model is that it can show how behaviours reinforce beliefs (deepest fears). Once a generic model has been formulated, a natural next step is to complete a thought challenging exercise (see next exercise).

Summary of uses:

- Clearly demonstrates self-defeating cycles.
- Excellent for socialising clients to the cognitive model.

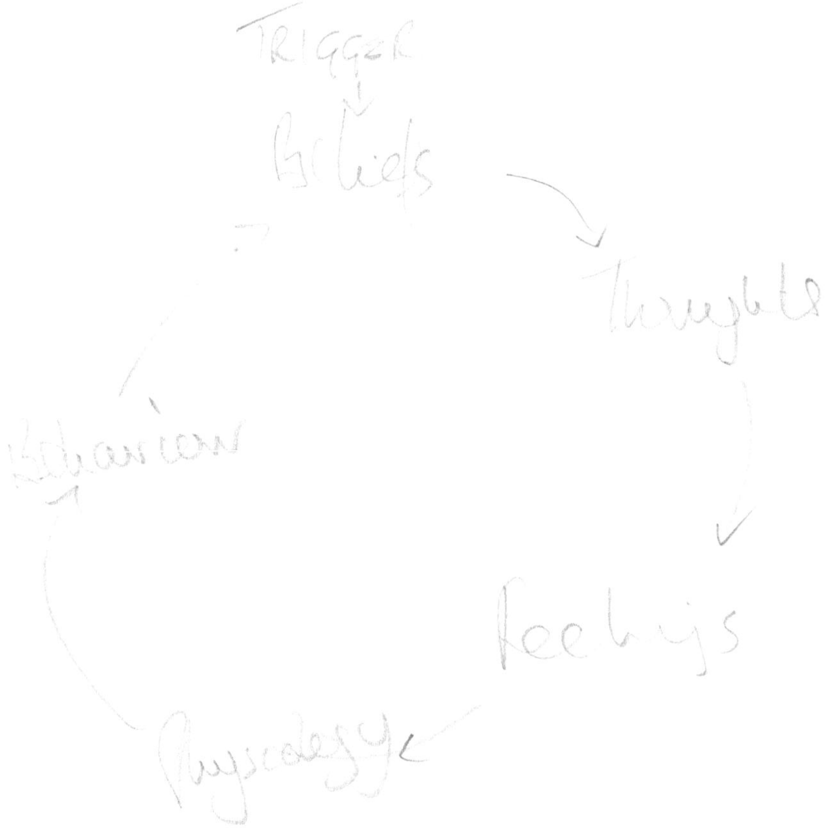

THE GENERIC CBT MODEL

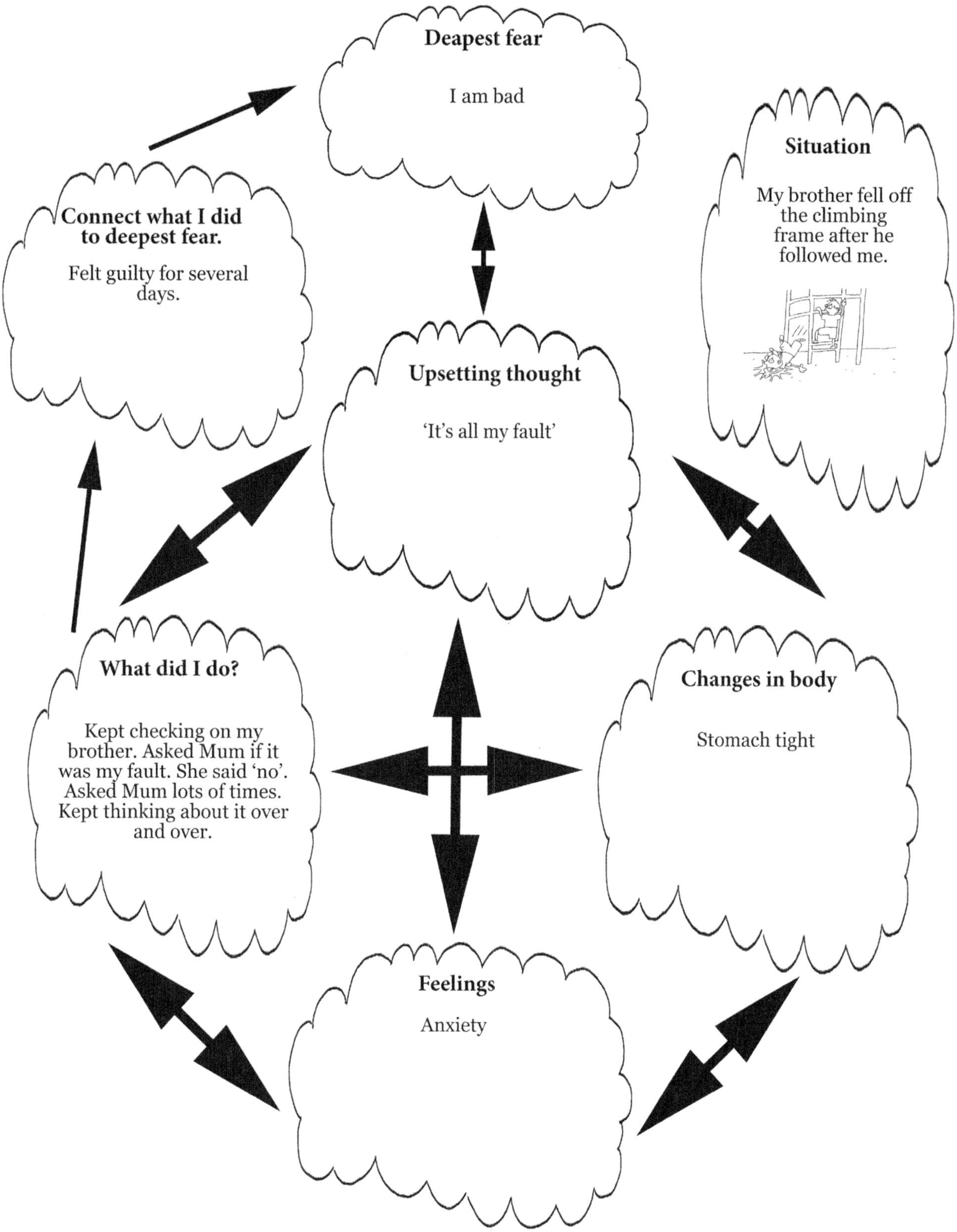

THE GENERIC CBT MODEL

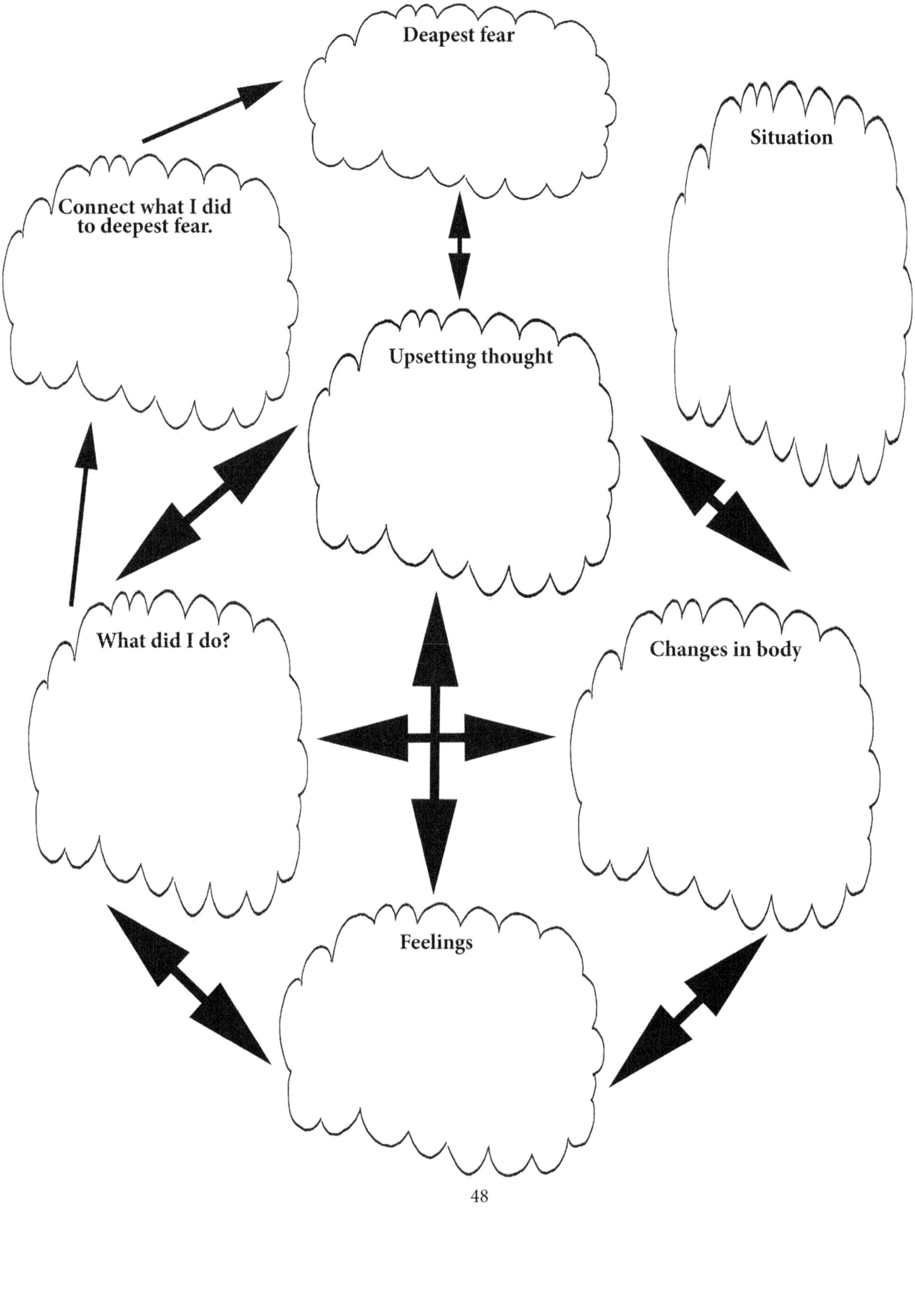

Creating balanced thoughts

Challenging negative automatic thoughts is the cornerstone of CBT. Ideally, the most distressing negative thought will be selected from your client's negative thoughts list. This can be achieved by asking your client to run through their negative thoughts mentally and to record how each thought makes them feel. The client can be asked to give each thought a 'Subjective Units of Distress Score' (SUDS) between 0 and 10 (where 10 is the most distressed they could possibly feel).

It is important when selecting a thought to avoid **beliefs** (unconditional and fixed ideas about the self). Beliefs (e.g., 'I am bad', 'I am worthless', 'I am unlovable') are best challenged using other exercises.

In the example on the next page we have selected the thought, 'It's all my fault' to work with. When challenging thoughts it is important to start with the 'evidence for' section. Asking your client to think of a prosecution lawyer can be helpful to generate ideas. When thinking of 'evidence for', any kind of evidence can be used. This will often be poor evidence driven by feelings, old memories, or internal critical suggestions. ('Evidence for' in this exercise is most likely to be associated with cognitive distortions rather than facts.) Once 'evidence for' has been exhausted only then move onto 'evidence against'. 'Evidence against' information can be evoked by using third-person strategies; for example, by asking your clients what trusted adults they know might say. The therapist can be quite active here, if necessary using guided discovery to help clients elicit ideas. Once evidence against the thought is exhausted it will then be time to move onto the next stage.

The fastest and most efficient way of creating a balanced thought is to summarise both 'evidence for' and 'evidence against' into a few words or a short sentence and to separate them using the word 'BUT'.

In our example, we have summarised the evidence for as 'I feel it was my fault that my brother hurt himself' and the evidence against as 'My parents are responsible for him, not me.' It can then be useful to ask your clients if both 'evidence for' and 'evidence against' parts agree on the new balanced thought. If agreement is achieved*, the client is then asked to run the new balanced thought through his/her mind and then re-rate his/her SUDS. If the client's SUDS have reduced, their balanced thought can then be inserted into a new positive generic CBT cycle. At this time, flash cards can also be created for clients to carry around that remind them of their new more balanced thoughts.

To obtain a new positive belief the therapist may ask, 'If the balanced thought [insert balanced, more accurate, thought here] is true, what would that say about you?'

*If agreement is not achieved, the exercise will need to be completed once more as there is likely to be missing information, or important thoughts may have been overlooked.

Summary of uses:

- Can be used to reduce distress associated with negative thoughts.
- Can be offered as homework.

CREATING BALANCED THOUGHTS

Situation

My brother fell off a climbing frame and hurt his arm.

Feelings

Anxiety

Negative thought

'It's all my fault'

Prosecution lawyer

Evidence for the thought

My brother followed me.
He would not have fallen off and hurt himself if I had not gone on the climbing frame.
I feel that it is my fault.
I feel bad.

Defence lawyer

Evidence against the thought

Mum and Dad said it wasn't my fault.
Accidents happen.
Mum and Dad said they should have been watching.
My brother did not listen to me when I said to go back to Mum and Dad.

New balanced thought

Summary of evidence for

I feel that it was my fault that my brother hurt himself,

but

Summary of evidence against

My parents are responsible for him, not me.

Judge

New feelings

More relaxed

CREATING BALANCED THOUGHTS

Situation

Feelings

Negative thought

Prosecution lawyer

Evidence for the thought

Defence lawyer

Evidence against the thought

New balanced thought

Summary of evidence for

but

Summary of evidence against

Judge

New feelings

Positive cycles

After creating a balanced thought, it is often very helpful to place it into a positive generic CBT cycle. This can create several benefits. It can: a) demonstrate to clients how they can change the way they feel by thinking differently; b) guide future behaviour, and c) show clients how changing their behaviour can reinforce new, more positive, beliefs.

Summary of uses:

- Guides future behaviour.
- Reduces distress.

MY POSITIVE CYCLE

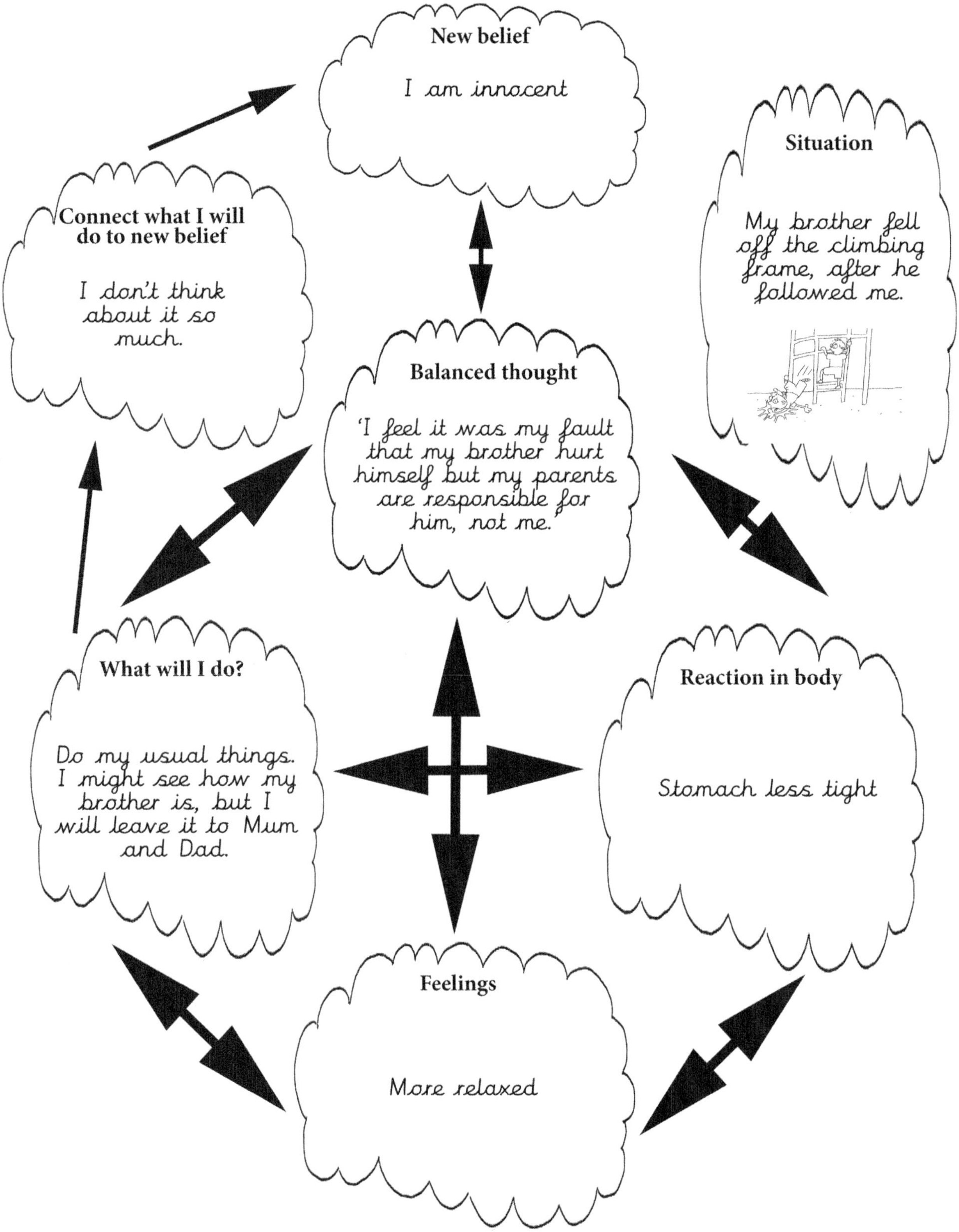

MY POSITIVE CYCLE

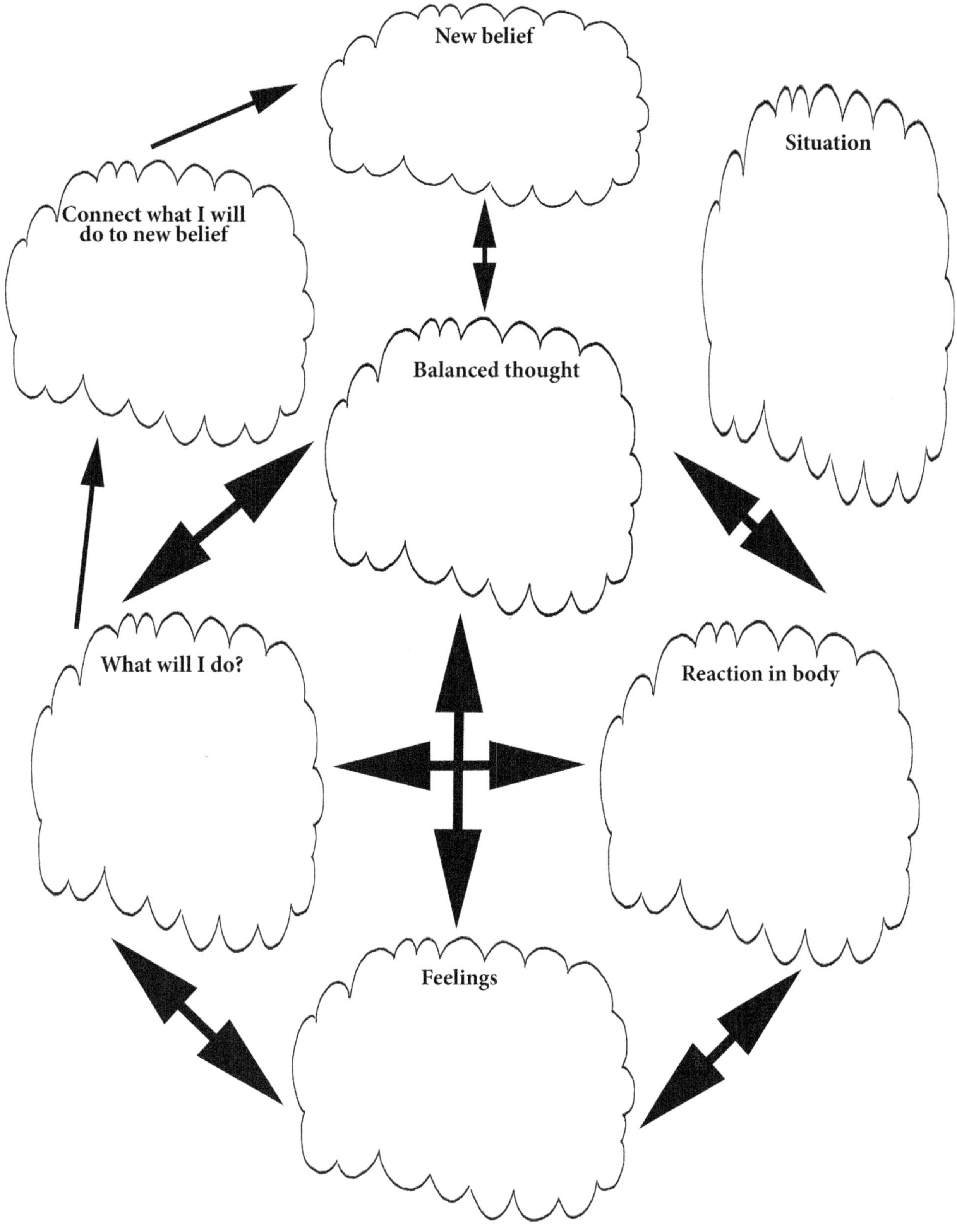

SECTION 5

Interventions

This section is dedicated to CBT interventions for OCD. Included for clinician use are worksheets for postponement, noticing intrusive thoughts, noticing habits, behavioural experiments, reducing a felt sense of responsibility, and creating a safe place. Ideally, clinicians will have had additional training in interventions, as interventions are often more complex than they might appear.

Benefits of this section:

- Brings client's awareness to the scale of the problems experienced.
- Helps to develop a problem list.
- Draws out intrusive thought content in a non-threatening way.
- Assists in the development of the therapist's initial formulation.
- Useful for homework exercises.
- Can assist in the development of collaboration between therapist and client.
- Encourages the development of goal-based behaviour.

Postponement

Postponement is a very powerful strategy for reducing neutralising behaviours. Depending on the situation clients are faced with, it is generally advisable to postpone for short periods initially and to then gradually extend the time periods. Prior to using postponement, clients will need to have learnt how to: a) stay with feelings (see the handout in the next section of this book), and b) respond to OCD urges (see urges handout).

Summary of uses:

- Reduces neutralising behaviour.
- Educates clients how to respond to OCD urges.
- Can be offered as homework.
- Increases child's sense of agency.
- Builds confidence.

Postponement

A very useful way to make OCD less powerful is to use postponement. This means that when your OCD tells you that you need to do something, you put it off to a later time.

First, pick an OCD behaviour that you want to do less of. Secondly, think about how you might feel at the time you decide not to do it. Finally, choose how you are going to respond to your OCD when the time comes to postpone your behaviour. You can use the boxes below to help you.

Write the behaviour you want to change in this box.

Phoning Mum to check where she is.

How will you feel when it comes to not completing this behaviour?

Very anxious.

How will you cope with these feelings?

Let my feelings in, as we practised.

What will you say to your OCD when you do not complete the behaviour? For example, 'I will do it in 30 minutes', 'I'll do it tonight'.

I'll give her a ring after I've done my homework.

Postponement

A very useful way to make OCD less powerful is to use postponement. This means that when your OCD tells you that you need to do something, you put it off to a later time.

First, pick an OCD behaviour that you want to do less of. Secondly, think about how you might feel at the time you decide not to do it. Finally, choose how you are going to respond to your OCD when the time comes to postpone your behaviour. You can use the boxes below to help you.

Write the behaviour you want to change in this box.

How will you feel when it comes to not completing this behaviour?

How will you cope with these feelings?

What will you say to your OCD when you do not complete the behaviour? For example, 'I will do it in 30 minutes', 'I'll do it tonight'.

What Happened When I Used Postponement?

A very useful way to help keep CBT strategies in place is to think about what happened when we tried something new. Fill out this sheet and give it to your therapist at your next session.

How did you feel when you used postponement?

I felt very anxious. The feeling kept going up and down.

What actually happened?

I kept wanting to phone Mum but I didn't. Mum came back before I finished my homework.

What did you learn from using postponement?

I knew I could check. I just didn't. I know checking can't change anything.

What Happened When I Used Postponement?

A very useful way to help keep CBT strategies in place is to think about what happened when we tried something new. Fill out this sheet and give it to your therapist at your next session.

How did you feel when you used postponement?

What actually happened?

What did you learn from using postponement?

Intrusive thoughts worksheet

This worksheet is designed to help children to expand their awareness of intrusive thoughts. Stepping back and observing intrusive thoughts is fundamental to a CBT approach to OCD. Writing down information about the thought encourages: a) increased detachment; b) curiosity and c) increased awareness that a thought is 'just a thought'.

Ideally, this sheet will be used in conjunction with the 'thought handout' sheet (see Section 6, page 134).

Summary of benefits:

- Helps to form a different relationship with thoughts.
- Introduces a mindfulness approach.
- Can be used as a homework exercise.
- Increases confidence and enhances choice.

Intrusive Thoughts Worksheet

Write or draw your intrusive thought in this box.

I'm going to be sick.

Write as much about the intrusive thought as possible. Was it an image or something else? How clear was it?

It was a really clear picture in my mind. I was sick on my classroom desk and everyone was looking at me.

Now place your thought in your 'thought safe'. You can also place this sheet in a jar with a lid or in a box that has a key.

Write how the thought made you feel here.

Feeling ill. I felt as though I uas going to be sick.

Intrusive Thoughts Worksheet

Write or draw your intrusive thought in this box.

Write as much about the intrusive thought as possible. Was it an image or something else? How clear was it?

Now place your thought in your 'thought safe'. You can also place this sheet in a jar with a lid or in a box that has a key.

Write how the thought made you feel here.

Breaking habits

Child clients may have built up a number of rituals and OCD habits without realising it. As such, it is really important to identify these habits in therapy. The essential component of breaking any habit is bringing it into conscious awareness. Once we have conscious awareness about what we are doing, it is only then that we have a choice. When we have a choice we can decide how to respond.

Summary of uses:

- Increases conscious awareness of automatic behaviours.
- Can be used as a homework exercise.

My Habits List

Use the box below to make a note of all of your habits. Habits are behaviours that you may complete without feeling any strong urges. Put as many things on your list as possible. Ask your parents or care givers for ideas as sometimes they may be able to spot things that you do not notice.

My habits list

1. Use tissue to lift up toilet seat.
2. Plump up pillows before I put my head on them.
3. Splash water over taps after I have used them.
4. Pull hair out of my eyebrows.
5. Look in the mirror to see how I look.
6. Check my phone when I don't need to.
7. Use my elbows to open doors.
8. Hold onto my lucky bracelet.
9. Fiddle with my hair.
10. Suck air through my teeth.

My Habits List

Use the box below to make a note of all of your habits. Habits are behaviours that you may complete without feeling any strong urges. Put as many things on your list as possible. Ask your parents or care givers for ideas as sometimes they may be able to spot things that you do not notice.

My habits list
1.
2.
3.
4.
5.
6.
7.
8.
9.
10.

Steps Involved in My OCD Habits

We complete habits without thinking about them. Some of our habits are very useful and they help us to complete things without thinking about it at all. However, some habits are not useful, especially if they are OCD habits. An important part of breaking an OCD habit is noticing that you are doing it. To help you with this, write down all of the steps involved.

1. Go into public restroom.
2. Wash my hands in the sink.
3. Push cubicle door open with my foot.
4. Take some tissue paper and use it to flush lavatory.
5. Use the lavatory.
6. Use tissue paper to flush lavatory.
7. Open the cubicle door using tissue paper.
8. Push the door open with my foot.
9. Throw tissue paper into lavatory as it is flushing.
10. Wash my hands in the sink.
11. Turn off taps with my elbows.
12. Walk out of restroom without touching anything. Open door handle using tissue paper.

Steps Involved in My OCD Habits

We complete habits without thinking about them. Some of our habits are very useful and they help us to complete things without thinking about it at all. However, some habits are not useful, especially if they are OCD habits. An important part of breaking an OCD habit is noticing that you are doing it. To help you with this, write down all of the steps involved.

1.

2.

3.

4.

5.

6.

7.

8.

9.

10.

11.

12.

Behavioural experiments

Changing behaviour is an essential part of CBT for OCD. Even if clients are able to change their thinking, their new way of thinking is unlikely to be embedded unless they also make associated behavioural changes. Behavioural experiments will help clients to develop new experiential understanding. This is likely to be one of the most important change aspects of their development as they progress through therapy.

Summary of uses:

- Develops experiential learning.
- Creates change very quickly.
- Can be used in sessions or as homework.
- Increases confidence.

OCD Experiment Record Sheet

Write down the behaviour you want to challenge in this box.

Asking Mum to check my heart.

How big is your OCD out of 100?

93

Write down what your new behaviour will be here.

Ignore what is happening with my heart.

What problems might you come up against when you complete your new behaviour? What might your OCD do and how will you overcome these problems?

I might feel anxious and worry about it. OCD will tell me that there is no harm in checking my heart. I will not listen to OCD.

What does OCD suggest will happen when you change your behaviour? Think of as many things that OCD might say as possible.

I could have a heart attack.

I will die suddenly.

It will be my fault.

NOW CHANGE YOUR BEHAVIOUR

What happened when you changed your behaviour?

I felt anxious for a while. I tried to think about other things instead. Somehow I forgot about my heart.

What did you learn from challenging your OCD? How big is your OCD now from 1 to 100, where 100 is the largest it can be?

I learnt that nothing happened.

89

OCD Experiment Record Sheet

Write down the behaviour you want to challenge in this box.

How big is your OCD out of 100?

Write down what your new behaviour will be here.

What problems might you come up against when you complete your new behaviour? What might your OCD do and how will you overcome these problems?

What does OCD suggest will happen when you change your behaviour? Think of as many things that OCD might say as possible.

NOW CHANGE YOUR BEHAVIOUR

What happened when you changed your behaviour?

What did you learn from challenging your OCD? How big is your OCD now from 1 to 100, where 100 is the largest it can be?

Responsibility pies

Responsibility pies are a very useful resource when working with clients who: a) have entrenched beliefs about being responsible; b) are taking too much responsibility for problems where a range of other people may be involved, and c) blame themselves for events that happened in the past or events that are happening in the present. The general idea is to make a list – as exhaustive as possible – of the people involved in a particular problem scenario. Work through the list, assigning how much percentage responsibility each person has for the problem, but remembering that it is essential to leave the client's percentage of responsibility until last. (This prevents clients allocating themselves too large a percentage of responsibility before they have considered the impact of others involved.)

Summary of benefits:

- Challenges an inflated sense of responsibility.
- Can be offered as homework.
- Helps clients to feel less alone.
- Useful for challenging 'fault-based' ideas.

Responsibility Pie Worksheet

Many people with OCD take on too much responsibility for things that are often not anything to do with them. This means that they feel that it is their fault if things go wrong and it's their job to fix other people's problems and to stop bad things from happening.

Using the list below write down all of the people involved in the issue that you are taking responsibility for. Decide how much of the pie you or they think they could have by circling a piece of pie next to their name. Leave yourself until last.

Using the pie on the next sheet, cut it up using scissors, giving a piece to everyone on your list who is involved. How much pie is left for you?

Describe what you feel responsible for here.

My brother, Paul, falling off a climbing frame and hurting his arm.

	100%	75%	50%	33%	25%	12.5%	0%
1. Mum							
2. Dad							
3. Paul							
4. Park Keeper							
5. Me							
6.							
7.							

Responsibility Pie Worksheet

Many people with OCD take on too much responsibility for things that are often not anything to do with them. This means that they feel that it is their fault if things go wrong and it's their job to fix other people's problems and to stop bad things from happening.

Using the list below write down all of the people involved in the issue that you are taking responsibility for. Decide how much of the pie you or they think they could have by circling a piece of pie next to their name. Leave yourself until last.

Using the pie on the next sheet, cut it up using scissors, giving a piece to everyone on your list who is involved. How much pie is left for you?

Describe what you feel responsible for here.

100% 75% 50% 33% 25% 12.5% 0%

1...

2...

3...

4...

5...

6...

7...

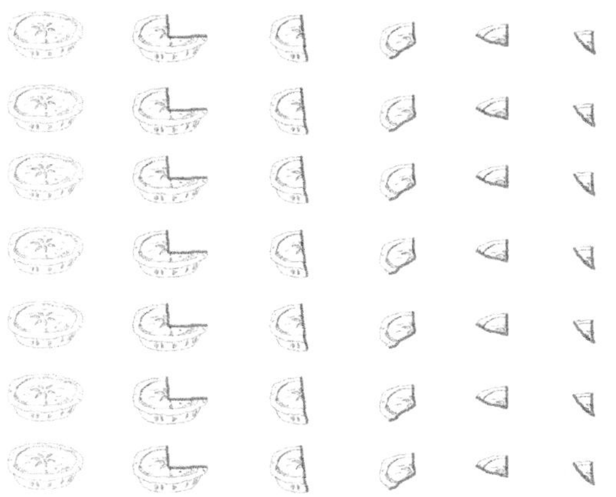

Responsibility Pie Worksheet

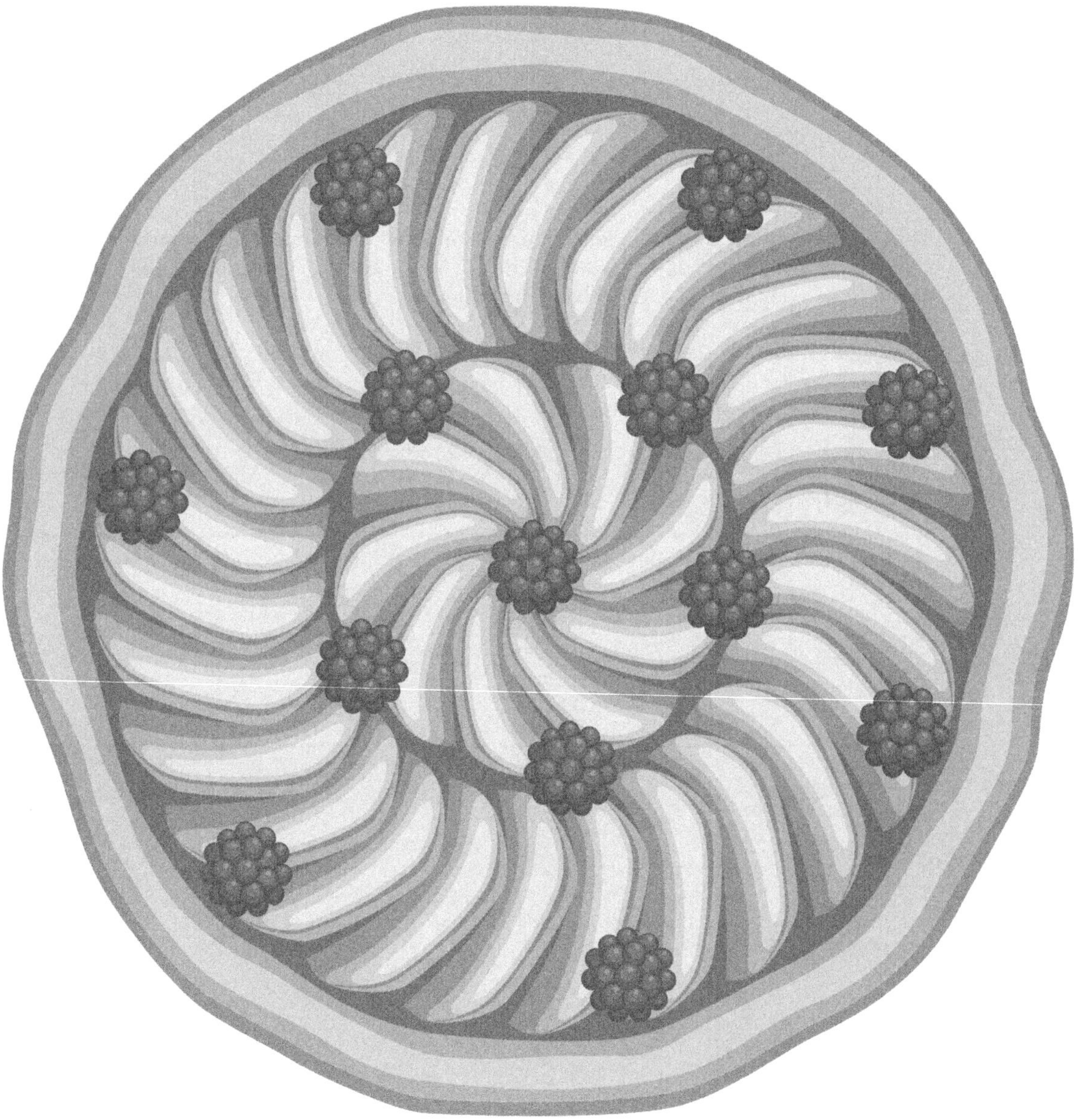

Safe place

A safe place is often a very useful exercise to complete with children who have high levels of anxiety.

It can be used to: a) bring anxiety levels down, and b) help clients to concentrate more effectively (as reduced anxiety levels result in improved attention, concentration and memory). Therapists can record information using the safe place template and make a copy to give to their clients to take away. The client can then read it, or the child's parent or carer can read it to their child if necessary.

Ideally, the safe place exercise will focus clients on all their sensory modalities, for example, 'What do you see?' 'What do you hear?' 'What do you smell?' 'How does the air feel against your skin?' This will help your clients to link their sensory modalities to one another, making the safe place more holistic and more memorable.

Beneficial questions can be asked by the therapist to draw out additional information. For example, if the child says, 'There is a river,' the therapist could ask, 'Is the river moving or still?' If the child says, 'It is moving,' the therapist could ask, 'What tells you from what you can see that it is moving?'

Summary of uses:

- Brings anxiety levels down.
- Can be used at the beginning of sessions to help improve concentration.
- Helps child clients to make a connection between therapy and feeling safe.
- Can be used by the child between sessions to reduce anxiety levels.

MY SAFE PLACE

Think of a place where you can go on your own. Ideally, this will not be a place that you already know. It will be an outdoor place where you feel safe and relaxed.

What would you like to call this place?

The river bank.

Look ahead at what you see. What do you notice?

I can see the book I am reading. I can see the water. I can see the grass.

Look to one side; what do you see?

I can see a fish swimming the water.

Look to the other side; what do you see there?

I can see grass. There are butterflies.

MY SAFE PLACE (2)

Listen to what you hear. What do you notice?

I can hear the sound of the river.

How do you feel when you hear these sounds?

I feel relaxed.

Breathe the air in this place. What is the air like to breathe?

It feels cool and fresh.

What does the air feel like on your skin? Where do you feel it?

Cool. On my face.

MY SAFE PLACE (3)

Feel the ground you are sitting or standing on. What does it feel like?

It feels soft and slightly cool.

Now notice what you see, what you hear, feel the air against your skin, the feeling of the ground underneath you. How do you feel?

Really relaxed.

If one word were to describe how you feel, what would that word be?

Relaxed

Say that word over and over in your mind. What is happening in your body?

It's starting to feel a little heavy. I could go to sleep.

MY SAFE PLACE

Think of a place where you can go on your own. Ideally, this will not be a place that you already know. It will be an outdoor place where you feel safe and relaxed.

What would you like to call this place?

Look ahead at what you see. What do you notice?

Look to one side; what do you see?

Look to the other side; what do you see there?

MY SAFE PLACE (2)

Listen to what you hear. What do you notice?

How do you feel when you hear these sounds?

Breathe the air in this place. What is the air like to breathe?

What does the air feel like on your skin? Where do you feel it?

MY SAFE PLACE (3)

Feel the ground you are sitting or standing on. What does it feel like?

Now notice what you see, what you hear, feel the air against your skin, the feeling of the ground underneath you. How do you feel?

If one word were to describe how you feel, what would that word be?

Say that word over and over in your mind. What is happening in your body?

Client handouts

Handouts can be very useful for clients and their parents to read between sessions, especially if large amounts of psycho-education need to be offered. In this section, we have included handouts that explain what OCD is, how thoughts work, how to respond to an OCD urge, how the brain works, and how to stay with emotions.

Benefits of this section:

- Gives clients an opportunity to absorb information in their own time.
- Enhances disclosure.

Joe goes to OCD school

Joe felt more nervous than usual as he walked up the path to his house. His mother had told him that morning that she wanted to have a chat with him when he got home from school.

'I'm not sure I feel up to having a chat today,' said Joe, as he walked through the front door.

'There's nothing to worry about, Joe,' said Joe's mum. 'I just wanted to have a talk with you about how things have been lately. We both know that you sometimes feel that you need to do certain things to stop yourself feeling uncomfortable. I've been reading about it on the internet and I think you have OCD!'

'What's OCD?' asked Joe.

'It stands for Obsessive Compulsive Disorder,' replied Joe's mum.

'Obsessive Compulsive Disorder. I don't understand! Is it something bad?' asked Joe.

Joe's mother put her arm around Joe's back and rubbed his shoulder. 'I don't think it's bad at all, but I don't want you to feel unhappy, so I would like you, Dad and I to visit an expert about it!'

'This definitely sounds serious!' thought Joe, hoping that his meeting with his mother was going to end as quickly as possible and that his mother would forget all about it.

'I don't need to see an expert! I think I'll be fine,' said Joe edging away from his mother.

'Of course you'll be fine, but let's think about what happened yesterday?' said Joe's mother smiling.

'Nothing happened yesterday!' whined Joe.

'With the mirror, remember?' replied Joe's mum. 'You kept going to the bathroom to check your mouth.'

'You seemed very worried and kept looking at your gums, and you were prodding inside your mouth. Then, after a while, you asked me to look inside your mouth because you were sure that you had cancer.'

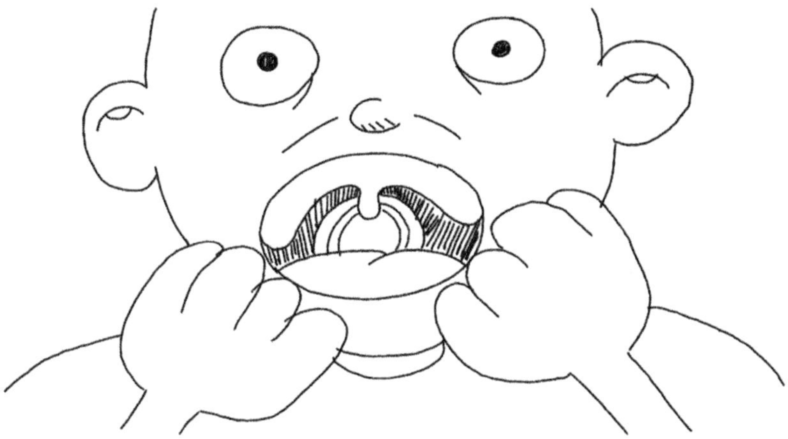

'But I'm not worried about that anymore. Don't you remember? You checked my mouth and it's all okay,' replied Joe.

'I know your mouth is okay, Joe, but it could be something else tomorrow,' said Joe's mother.

'I don't know what you mean,' groaned Joe.

'Over the past few weeks you have been looking very closely at your food and refusing to eat a lot of things,' suggested Joe's mother.

'Yes, but there's a good reason for that. It's because the food might have germs on it. I found out at school that germs are everywhere, and germs make people sick,' replied Joe.

'If I think about all the things that I have touched it makes me feel like I'm going to be ill. You remember that time I was sick, don't you!' continued Joe.

'Yes. I remember when you were sick. It happened years ago, when you were three,' said Joe's mother.

'I guess your worries about germs explain why I found you in the shower washing yourself with disinfectant,' said Joe's mother.

'No, I wasn't washing myself with it. I was washing the shower!' said Joe. 'The label says it kills all known germs.'

'In any case, I feel that you're just not happy any more, and I want some help to make sure I'm doing the right things. I'd like you to come with me to OCD school,' said Joe's mother.

'Can I think about it?' muttered Joe.

'Yes, you can think about it, Joe, but I don't think thinking about it is going to help us. I've found out that there's an OCD school really close by. I think it will be worth us looking! We don't have to do anything. I just want to see if they can help. That's all!'

'Okay,' said Joe, quietly.

Jo visits OCD school

The days passed quickly and the time soon came for Joe and his parents to go to OCD school.

'It looks like a nice building...maybe it won't be too bad,' thought Joe, as they reached the outside.

Once through the door they found a waiting room, with a few children sitting down waiting for their appointments. Joe and his parents were there for only a few minutes when a man wearing glasses approached them.

'You must be Joe,' said the man smiling. 'I'm Dr Jones. I help people understand and cope better with OCD. Please come this way, then you, Mum and Dad can tell me all about it.'

When they were inside Dr Jones' office, Dr Jones turned to Joe and said, 'Okay, Joe, it's great to see you, so tell me what's been happening?'

'I'm not really sure,' said Joe, nuzzling his head into his mother's armpit. 'Can Mum tell you?'

'Sure!' said Dr Jones.

Joe's mother had come prepared. She reached into her handbag and brought out a notebook with lots of her thoughts about Joe written in it.

'There are quite a few things I'd like to tell you about why we have come to OCD school today,' said Joe's mum. 'Joe has always liked things being in order.... He lines things up.... He tries to make sure that spaces between things are the same before he does anything. If he sees hangers facing different ways he wants to rearrange them.'

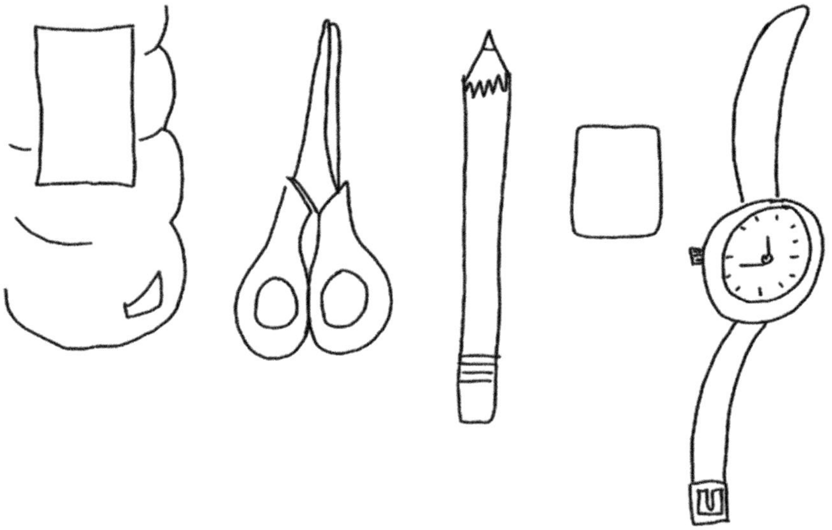

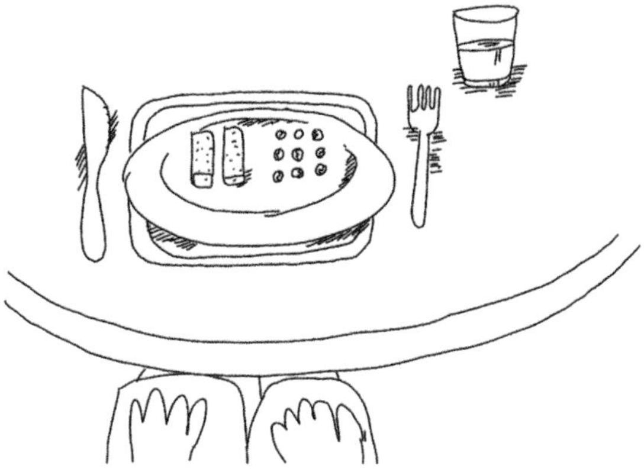

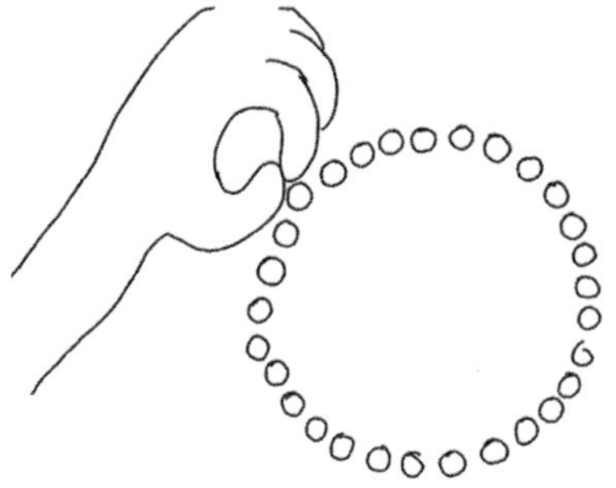

'Joe sometimes likes to arrange his food before he eats it, and he moves his food around to make perfect shapes. Joe doesn't like it if his brother opens his crisps the wrong way around or if people have dirty clothes. Joe has always been like that. Joe's grandmother is the same way, so it's probably something that runs in the family.'

‘Over the past few months we have noticed that Joe doesn’t seem his happy self any more. He has been taking too much responsibility for others, worrying about his friends and having thoughts that bad things might happen to them.’

‘Joe has also started feeling more nervous in the evening, especially when it starts to get dark. He has been finding it difficult to sleep at night.’

'Joe has been carrying out several behaviours that he feels he has to do before he goes to bed. He says he must do everything in the same order, or he needs to start again from the beginning,' said Joe's mum, turning to the next page in her notebook.

'I have to touch my lamp three times, blink three times, and then cross my arms across my chest,' said Joe, seizing an opportunity to interrupt his mother.

Joe's mother looked concerned and shook her head.

'I would just like to add that Joe does it over and over again. This can mean that he goes to sleep very late and he feels very tired when he wakes up in the morning,' said Joe's mum.

Joe's mother continued quickly, 'Joe also seems to be very worried about his health at the moment. He keeps checking himself in the mirror, taking his pulse and feeling his chest.'

'I think Joe's worried that he's going to have a heart attack,' said Joe's mother.

'Is there anything happening in Joe's life that may have led to an increase in Joe's behaviours?' asked Dr Jones, attempting to get to the root of Joe's problem.

'Well! He does have a new teacher who shouts a lot and I think Joe has been worried that he will shout at him.'

'Since he's had this new teacher he seems to spend a lot of his time on homework doing the same work over and over again. He can spend hours on it,' replied Joe's mum.

'Have you noticed any other behaviours that Joe carries out that concern you?' asked Dr Jones.

'Joe sometimes retraces his steps and he goes back the same way he has already come. He tries to avoid walking on cracks in the pavement and will cross the road if he notices paving slabs with lots of cracks in them.'

'Joe worries a lot when I go out. He usually calls me lots of times and leaves messages asking if I am okay. When I looked at my phone last week after the cinema, there were about 20 text messages from him asking me where I was,' said Joe's Mum.

After a little while, Joe's mum had finished telling Dr Jones about Joe's OCD. She closed her notebook, looked hopefully at Dr Jones and said, 'Is this something you can help us with?'

Dr Jones paused and thought quietly for a moment before speaking.

'Joe certainly has an OCD problem. From the look of it, it has grown quite large! It's an interesting creature. It seems strong and powerful. It's got some features that make it quite original, which is often the case with OCD. There's no need to worry though, Joe. Once we start to learn about OCD together you'll soon have it sorted. It's not the biggest case of OCD I've seen. I've seen cases of OCD where whole families have been involved in trying to manage it.'

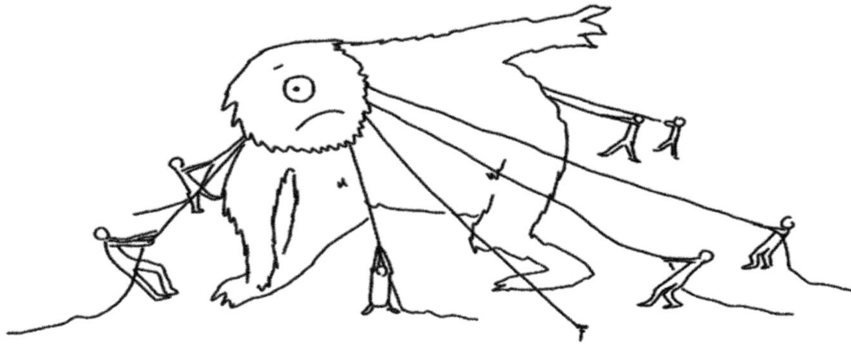

‘What is OCD? Why me?’ asked Joe with a sad tone in his voice.

‘OCD simply means Obsessive Compulsive Disorder. **Obsessive** means that we can literally feel taken over by certain thoughts, feelings and sensations. **Compulsive** means that we feel compelled to act or behave in a certain way. It feels like we have no choice,’ replied Dr Jones. He got up from his seat to point at his white board. ‘For many people there can be different things that make OCD a problem, but in most cases it’s **genetic**. By genetic, I mean it runs in families and people are born that way. I’ll talk about it in a little more detail now,’ said Dr Jones.

'There is a part of the brain that is supposed to act as a gatekeeper. Its job is to prevent thoughts that are not real or not important entering the mind. In people with OCD, this part of the brain falls asleep a lot and lets in all kinds of thoughts that aren't really allowed in. This means that people with OCD can have more frightening thoughts than others without it. The most compelling or strongest thoughts in OCD are called '**intrusive thoughts**'. These thoughts can feel very real and frightening. They are often thoughts that tell us that

people have been hurt or injured, or that something terrible has happened or will happen to ourselves or others.

'It is like living in a nightmare; intrusive thoughts really feel that frightening. People with OCD struggle with their intrusive thoughts and will often carry out behaviours to try to make them feel less frightening in an attempt to calm themselves down. It's a little like watching a horror movie on the TV.'

'You try to turn off the TV, but the remote control doesn't work. Pulling out the TV cable doesn't work either. The horror film stays on no matter what you do! Sometimes it can get so bad you get sucked into the horror film. You feel stuck and it feels very frightening, as if there is no way out. No one else seems to understand just how terrible it is.'

'Because of their high levels of fear, many people with OCD carry out **neutralising behaviours**. Neutralising behaviours are things that people do, often several times, to help reduce the intensity of the feelings that they experience. For you, Joe, this has led to you carrying out **rituals** at night. Rituals are the things you do over and over again, like touching your lamp three times and doing things in the same order. Sometimes people have completed rituals for so long that they are no longer aware they are doing them. They can become very upset if they're prevented from carrying them out,' said Dr Jones.

'What do you think has made Joe's problem get worse just recently?' asked Joe's Mum.

'It could be changes in his life. Growing up can also lead to OCD becoming more of a problem. At the moment, though, I think it's around Joe finding it difficult to get used to his new teacher,' said Dr Jones.

'For most people with OCD, it starts off in a very small way. It makes little suggestions about what you can do to feel a little better. For example, it might say, "Just go and wash your hands, Joe, and you'll be clean.... Don't put that there, put it here, that'll be best.... Let's just check that – just in case – it's better to be safe than sorry." These things work at first, so we start listening to it a little more.'

‘It carries on making suggestions, here and there. It’s only trying to make us feel better.’

‘It seems like a helpful little voice that simply wants to make us feel a little safer and a nice person.’

‘But the more we listen to it, the bigger, more powerful and out of control it seems to become.’

'After a while, it feels like it's bigger than we are. It's in charge and we feel like we need to do what it says.'

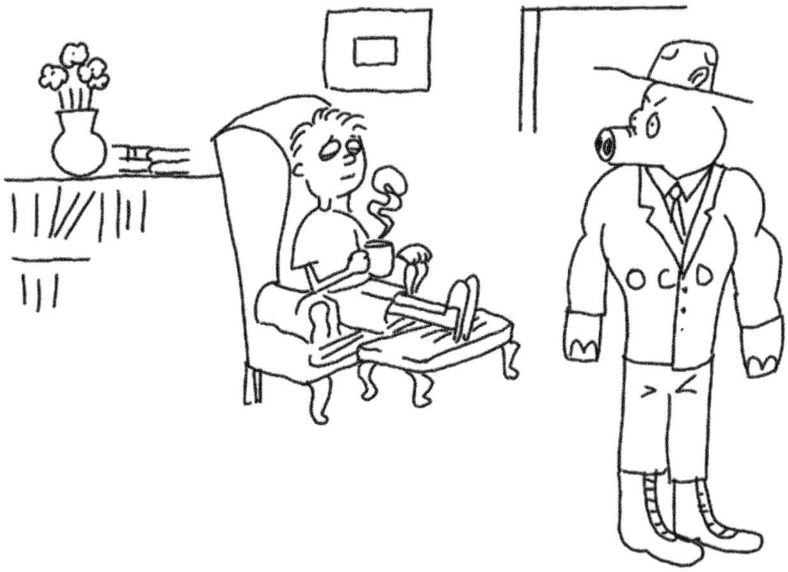

'There starts to become less time for ourselves as OCD tells us that more things need to be done to keep ourselves or others safe and to be a good person'.

‘While we’re doing all of these things to feel safe and good, it only works for a while. We may have more frightening intrusive thoughts about bad things happening; for example, Mum and Dad being in an accident. These thoughts can feel very real and clear.’

'For you, Joe, your OCD might suggest that you should check to see if Mum or Dad are okay. If you can't find them straight away this can feel very frightening. Not immediately knowing that Mum or Dad are okay leads to more frantic checking. This makes you feel more panicky and frightened. Feeling more frightened, you believe Mum or Dad must be unsafe. Sometimes, when it gets really bad, you may actually think it's your fault that Mum or Dad might not be okay and that you've done something wrong. Of course, this isn't true but that's what it feels like.'

'Of course, when Mum eventually looks at her phone and sees multiple texts asking her where she is, she feels very surprised and shocked.'

'Intrusive thoughts make us feel highly anxious. This creates a problem because the more anxious we feel, the more frequent our intrusive thoughts become.'

‘In states of high anxiety, we feel that we need to check more things to be safe. If we do it enough times, checking or rituals can become habits that we feel we have to do, and we can’t relax until we feel that we’ve done them right.’

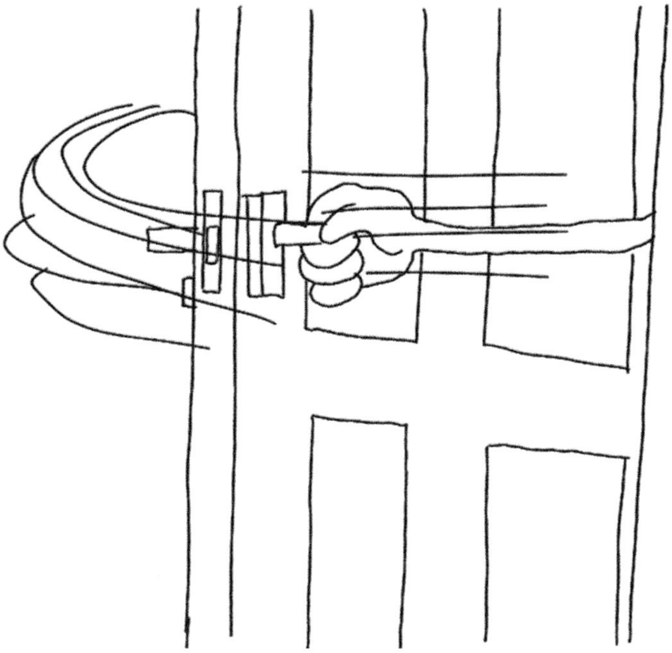

'It can seem like OCD's voice is very strong in our minds and we don't know what to do to make things feel better like they were once before,' said Dr Jones.

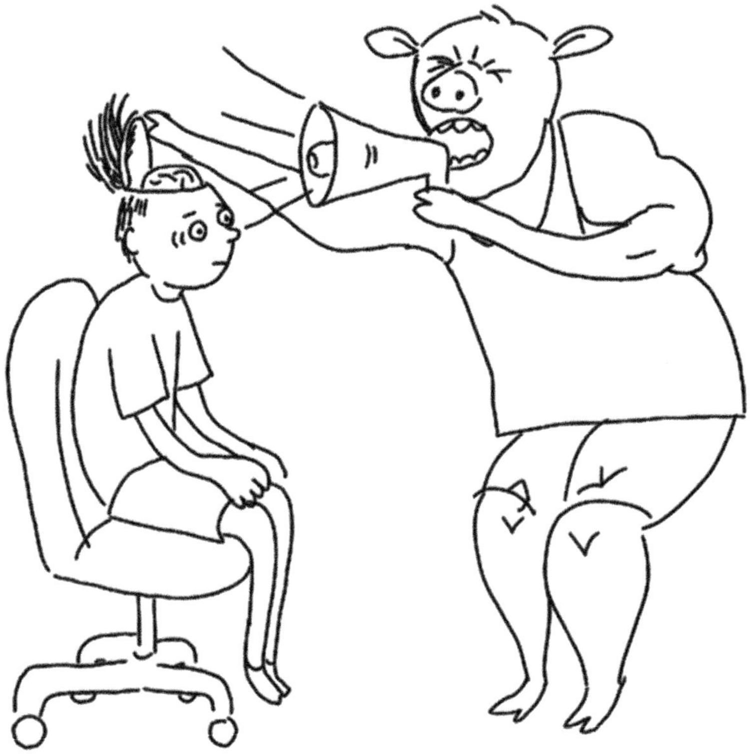

Joe concentrated intensely on Dr Jones' feedback. It was as if Dr Jones could see exactly what life was like for him.

'So, what can we do to make things feel better for Joe and to help him with his OCD? Is there anything that my husband George and I need to be doing?' asked Joe's mother.

'Well. That's where there is some good news!' said Dr Jones, rolling up his sleeves. 'There's a lot we can do to help Joe with his OCD. The first thing I'd like to share with you is that we can change how powerful OCD is just by recognising that it's there. In the world outside there are lots of people with OCD. Everyone's OCD is slightly different and for some it's a bigger problem than for others.'

'Some people can live their whole life with OCD without really recognising that it's there and not getting any help. For others, it can help them with their work, and they get good results at school.'

'But for many people it can become a problem, especially if they start to feel very unhappy and it gets in the way of them living their life. In the waiting room you will have seen children whose OCD is at different levels. The more they work on their OCD using the ideas we teach at this school, the smaller their OCD becomes.'

'I had quite an OCD problem myself as a child. It made me feel that I needed to do all kinds of different things. I didn't feel in charge of my life.'

'Now it's not such a big problem because I can see it for what it is. I always show it kindness and thank it for its suggestions. I just don't do what it says any more.'

‘I keep an eye on it and bring it out from time to time to see how I’m doing with it.’

‘It’s hard not to do what OCD says when it’s big and powerful, but there are many things we can do to listen to it less.’

‘The less we act on what it says the smaller it becomes. Sometimes it can take quite a while to shrink; because OCD thinks it has been keeping you safe, and for that reason it doesn’t like to give up.’

'One day Joe, as you learn to listen and react less to your OCD, you'll find that your OCD gets smaller and smaller as well.'

'A good starting point in managing your OCD will be forming a different type of relationship with your feelings, especially fear and anxiety, instead of listening to what OCD tells you to do to feel better.'

'OCD normally suggests that you hide from anxiety and that you should carry out behaviours to get rid of it. But at OCD school we learn to form a new relationship with emotions that are upsetting and frightening.'

'We can practise staying with feelings now if you'd like?' asked Dr Jones, turning to look directly at Joe.

Joe fidgeted in his chair. He had begun to feel slightly nervous, as he wasn't keen on trying new things.

'Dr Jones has got his OCD to be really tiny, Joe. Maybe it could work for you as well!' said Joe's Mum, trying to reassure Joe.

'Okay! I'll give it a go,' said Joe, sitting up in his chair.

'Right, Joe,' said Dr Jones. 'Let's start with you having a think about something that might make you feel very anxious. How about the teacher who shouts a lot in class?'

'I'm not sure I want to think about that,' said Joe.

'That's okay, Joe, you don't need to be sure, we can just give it a go,' said Dr Jones.

'Okay, I'll think about him shouting,' muttered Joe.

'Well done, Joe, that's really courageous,' said Joe's mother.

'How are you feeling?' asked Dr Jones.

'Not great!' said Joe.

'I feel dizzy!' Joe whispered to his mother.

'Where do you feel it?' asked Dr Jones.

'In my head,' said Joe.

'How about in your body?' asked Dr Jones.

'It's mainly in my tummy and in my chest,' replied Joe, squirming.

'You're being very brave, Joe, noticing your feelings,' said Dr Jones. 'Keep feeling your feelings. I know it doesn't feel very nice, but stay with it. Make space for your feelings and let them be.'

‘What’s happening to your feeling now?’ asked Dr Jones.

‘It still feels uncomfortable but it’s getting smaller and less spiky,’ said Joe as he started to relax.

‘Now it’s getting even smaller. I can hardly feel it at all,’ continued Joe.

‘What do you make of that?’ asked Dr Jones.

‘That’s very strange. I’ve never tried that before!’ said Joe.

‘Would you like to come with me to take a tour of the school, so we can show you what else we do here, Joe?’ suggested Dr Jones.

‘Yes,’ said Joe. ‘I guess I could take a look.’

Joe tours OCD school

Joe followed Dr Jones down the corridor until Dr Jones stopped outside a door marked 'Lists'.

'OK, Joe! This is one of the first classes that our students go to. It's called the 'Making a List' class. In this class, students make a list of all the things that they feel that their OCD makes them do to help them feel safe. We refer to the things written on these lists as '**safety behaviours**'. We usually encourage our students to make their list as long as possible to make sure that nothing is left out. Some students have short lists, others have very long lists. Usually, if students have larger OCD problems their list of safety behaviours is longer.

'Lists are very useful to our students. Students can look through their lists and decide where they want to start reacting differently to their OCD. To reduce the power of their OCD, students will usually begin by dropping safety behaviours that they feel will be the easiest to drop.

'We'll go to see a few more classes now so you can see what else we do,' said Dr Jones.

Joe and Dr Jones walked down the corridor a little further until they reached a room labelled 'Postponement', at which point Dr Jones paused.

'Right, Joe. In this class we practise putting off what OCD asks us to do. For example, if OCD says that you need to wash your hands straight away because you've just had a thought about germs or something, you tell OCD "thank you" and that you'll wash them later. You might say to your OCD, "I'll do it in half an hour" or "I'll wash them this evening".

'OCD is very impatient and doesn't like to wait. Waiting is a very important tool for making OCD smaller and less powerful. Each time we wait, OCD is no longer running our lives. We start to have more choice about what we want to do in our lives.'

‘We’ll move on to the next class now, Joe,’ said Dr Jones as he turned and walked out of the postponement class. Joe followed him up a flight of stairs. At the top of the stairs was a room with a label on it saying ‘Experiments in Progress’.

‘What kinds of experiments do the children do?’ whispered Joe.

‘Many different types,’ replied Dr Jones. ‘In this room, students ask their OCD what it thinks is going to happen if they don’t complete a safety behaviour. Then the student deliberately doesn’t complete the safety behaviour to see what actually happens. This can be quite frightening, as at first our students’ OCD can be very convincing, making them believe that something really bad is going to happen and it will be their fault!

‘My OCD used to tell me that I should avoid going to church. This is because I once had a thought that I was going to burst into flames if I went into a church. I was frightened when I first went in, thinking it might happen, but of course nothing happened,’ said Dr Jones.

Dr Jones looked at his watch. 'Okay. That's enough time spent here. I think it's time to go to the next room now, Joe,' said Dr Jones.

Joe followed Dr Jones as he walked down two curling sets of stairs to the building's basement. Joe soon found himself in front of a large black metal door with a label written on it that said 'Silence! Work with intrusive thoughts in progress'.

'Right, Joe,' whispered Dr Jones. 'This is quite an advanced class. In this class, students need to concentrate very hard as they learn how to spot and respond to intrusive thoughts differently. Students remind themselves that their intrusive thoughts are thoughts just like any other thoughts.'

'In the early stages of this class, our students may practise putting their thoughts into an imaginary safe with a lock on it until they feel confident enough to deal with them. That way students can take them out later one at a time and work with them.'

'After a while it becomes easier not react to intrusive thoughts quite as much.'

'Okay. I think it's time for us to move on now. There's still quite a lot left to see,' said Dr Jones.

Joe and Dr Jones walked down the corridor a little further until Dr Jones stopped and pointed at a sign on a door that said 'REMEMBER! NO CHATTING' in big red letters.

'Do the students talk to each other too much in this class?' whispered Joe.

'No! It's not to stop our students talking to each other. It's a reminder to our students about how to respond to their OCD,' said Dr Jones, chuckling. 'OCD continually tries to grab our students' attention, so we teach our students to spend less time chatting with it. When students refuse to complete safety behaviours, their OCD often becomes noisy, trying to get attention. It makes suggestions about why the safety behaviour is important. It tries to convince our students to do what it wants. If it realises that it's not going to get what it wants, it then tries to **negotiate**.'

'Negotiate?' enquired Joe.

'Yes,' said Dr Jones, clearing his throat. 'Let's say, for example, you've decided that you're not going to wash your hands at school unless you need to visit the toilets. OCD might say "That's OK as long as you wiped your hands with anti-bacterial gel in the morning." OCD will often try to negotiate if you say no to it. It rarely just gives up. The key to making OCD even smaller is not to chat with it and to decline its offer to negotiate. Perhaps saying something like "No thanks, I'm happy with my choices".'

'We'll go to the class next door now where students are working on breaking their habits,' said Dr Jones.

Seconds later, Joe was looking into the classroom. The children were deliberately going through their OCD behaviours and writing down the steps involved in their habits. One girl looked as if she was thinking through a process of pulling on her eyelashes.

'Here the students are making a note of their habits in some detail. OCD might have encouraged them to pick up habits in the past and many of our students carry out OCD habits without thinking. The key to breaking habits is to notice that we are doing them. Once we bring a habit to mind we feel as if we have more choice about whether we want to carry out the habit or not. Breaking OCD habits is one way that students can reduce the size of their OCD.

'Do you like making pies, Joe?' asked Dr Jones.

'Making pies?' asked Joe, looking at Dr Jones quizzically.

'We're going to our pie class next door now. Our pie classes are to stop our students taking on too much responsibility for things in their lives,' said Dr Jones.

'People with OCD have an **overinflated sense of responsibility**. This means that they feel that it is their fault if things go wrong and it's their job to fix other people's problems and to stop bad things from happening. The truth is that people often have much less responsibility for things than they think they do. This is especially the case for children.

'In this class, our students make a pie and they give a slice to everyone who they can share responsibility with.'

'I don't think I understand,' said Joe hesitantly.

'Well, let's imagine that your younger brother falls off a climbing frame in the park. You are with him and shout to him to be careful, but he doesn't listen. He falls and hurts his arm and you feel that it's your fault because you are the older brother. He was trying to follow you and he didn't listen when you said to go back.'

‘If you were in this class, we would create a responsibility pie for you. After you have your pie in front of you, we then decide who to give slices to and how big each slice could be. We could give a piece of pie to your brother, a piece of pie to your mum and dad who weren’t looking, a piece to the park keeper who was on his phone instead of watching. At the end you might find that there may be only a tiny little piece left for you. When unfortunate things or accidents happen there are often lots of people involved. To truly find out why anything happens we’d have to go back to the beginning of time itself! That makes your part in the event pretty tiny,’ said Dr Jones.

‘I think we’ll make our final stop in the meditation class next door,’ said Dr Jones. ‘In this class, students spend time watching their thoughts and learn to separate themselves from their thoughts. This is very helpful for students with OCD as it helps them to develop clearer minds. With clearer minds our students feel more relaxed.

‘Through meditation, students learn how to move their attention away from OCD worrying thoughts and choose to trust instead. At first, they need quite a lot of help with this, but it usually results in OCD getting smaller and smaller. There are lots of different ways to do meditation. Some students imagine their thoughts on a conveyor belt and watch them as they go by.’

‘Others imagine putting their thoughts on leaves and watch them as they float away.’

'Okay, Joe,' said Dr Jones, turning to look at Joe. 'I think I've shown you most of what we do here. There are many other things we do as well, but I think you've seen enough for your first day. Most people with OCD have their own one-to-one teachers. At our school we call them therapists. We'll fix you up with one if you decide you'd like to come back.'

'Thank you,' said Joe. 'I'll ask my Mum and Dad.'

'Let's go and find Mum and Dad now,' said Dr Jones.

Joe followed Dr Jones as they went up the stairs. Joe smiled when he saw his parents. He did not feel so alone with his OCD any more. He didn't know why, but he felt that somehow things were going to be better in the future.

Joe thinks about his OCD

In the car on the way home, Joe felt tired but happier and less weighed down.

'Mum... Dad... I think I might like to go to OCD school, if that's okay,' said Joe.

'Of course,' said Joe's father.

'We'd like to go as well,' said Joe's mother. 'We found out that there's a parents' class there. We discovered that parents can sometimes make their children's OCD worse, especially if they do things to help their children do what their OCD wants. We learnt that although parents are not supposed to stop children doing their OCD behaviours, parents must also not assist their children with the completion of OCD behaviours and rituals. Apparently, helping your children to complete their OCD behaviours can make their OCD grow to a huge size,' continued Joe's Mum.

Joe imagined his OCD sitting next to him. 'I know you're with me, and I'm pleased to make your acquaintance. I'm looking forward to "seeing you" more. But I'm going to show you that I am the one who is really in charge,' thought Joe.

Use this section to write down what you think Joe learned about OCD by going to OCD school

THOUGHTS HANDOUT

Thoughts come in all shapes and sizes.

Thoughts can be about all manner of subjects. They can be like pictures in our heads or words in our heads. They can come into our minds quickly or slowly. They can be really clear or they can be faint and difficult to notice. We can even have thoughts about our own thoughts, for example, 'Wow, I'm having a lot of thoughts today' or 'I have no thoughts. My mind is blank'.

We can have thoughts about what is happening in our lives, what we want, and things that we think that we need to do.

We can have thoughts about things that make us laugh.

THOUGHTS HANDOUT - Page 2

We can have thoughts that make us cry.

We can have thoughts that are a little like bullies. They barge their way into our minds when we are not expecting them. They feel very real and frightening when they come in. We call these intrusive thoughts.

We can have thoughts that keep coming back like a boomerang. We try to push them out and they keep coming back.

However ... It is important to remember that all thoughts, no matter how frightening, exciting, boring, or repetitive, are just suggestions by the mind. It is important to notice our thoughts, but also to recognise that not every thought needs to be dealt with. We can choose to respond to our thoughts or we can choose to let them go.

HOW TO RESPOND TO AN OCD URGE

It is difficult challenging an OCD behaviour as at first the urge to do it will feel particularly strong.

If you are able to stay with that urge and not complete the OCD behaviour the urge feeling is likely to increase first and then gradually decrease as time passes. Your OCD will not give up after the first wave of compulsive feeling has passed. The urge feeling usually returns a little while later and you may find yourself feeling that you want to go back and complete the behaviour. At this time it is important to notice the thought, label the feeling, and wait.

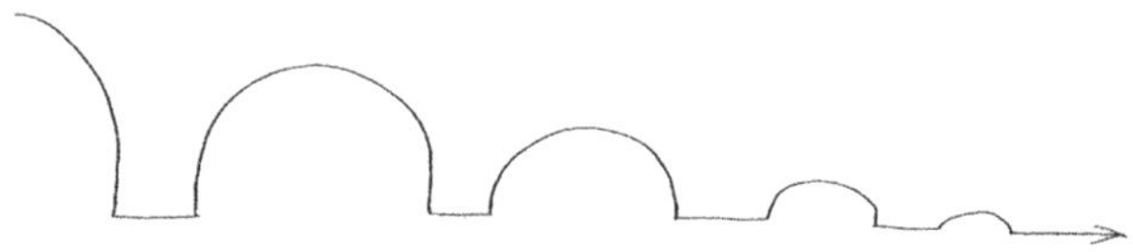

If you wait and stay with your urges as they pass, you will find that the urge ripples get smaller and smaller until they eventually vanish.

After this it is important not to add any further OCD behaviours. OCD doesn't like to give up and will usually try to come back with something else.

HOW JOE CREATES CHECKING HABITS

Joe feels upset because he thinks he has mouth cancer

Joe starts to feel highly anxious

Joe asks his mother to check his mouth

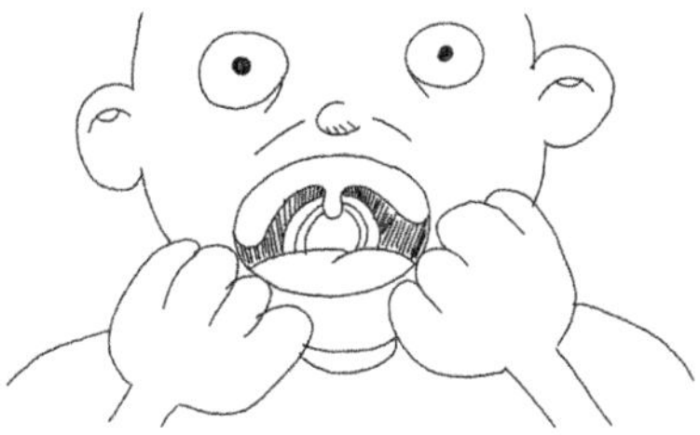

After his mother checks his mouth Joe's anxiety goes away.

Joe finds that having his mother check things leads to him feeling less anxious, so he asks her to check things more often.

Brain organisation

BIG JIM: There are three parts to the brain that you will find out about when you do CBT. The clever part is based at the top of the brain.

The clever part is good at doing difficult things like crosswords, mathematics, homework and solving problems.

At the bottom of the brain is the animal part.

The animal part is very loyal, a bit like my dog, but is also pretty stupid and believes everything that you tell it. It is in charge of feelings so we need to be careful with it.

There is another little part in between the clever part and the animal part. It sorts out problems between the two of them. This part is the 'minder'.

The minder helps the brainy part sort out the animal when it gets a bit upset or angry. The minder is very good at calming down the animal part and can manage it, if it gets upset.

Overall the brain looks something like this picture.

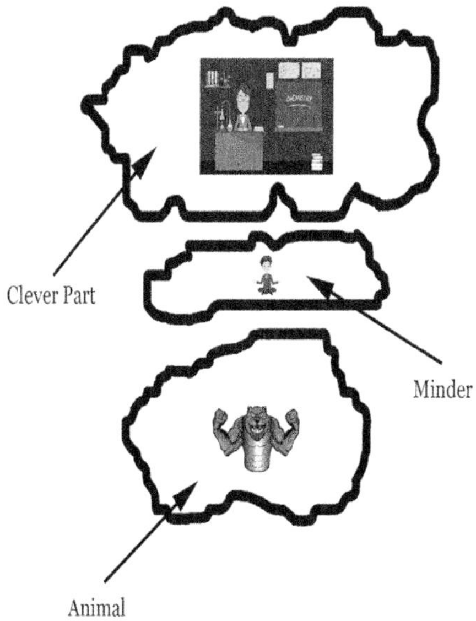

SALLY: Professor Nut. Do you have anything to add about what people might find out about the brain?

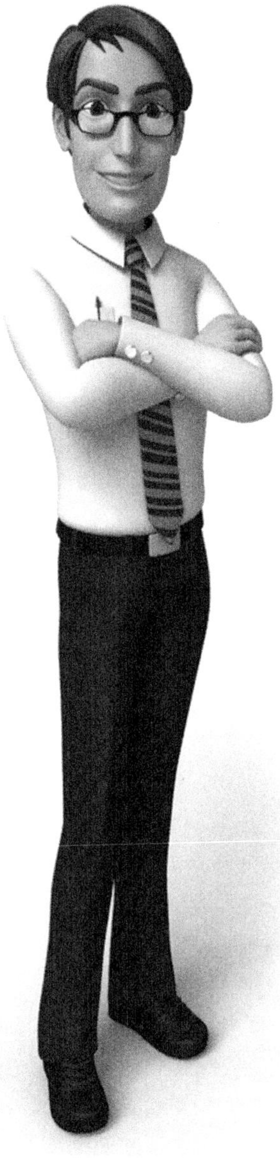

PROFESSOR NUT: Have a look at my diagram below. If you look at the brain from the top down everything that you can see on the surface is called the neocortex. The neocortex is a part of the brain that we use to think, plan and solve complex problems. You will need to use this part of the brain quite a bit when you do CBT. The lower areas of the brain that reside underneath the neocortex are known by people in my field as subcortical regions. The subcortical regions could be described as the primitive or animal brain, as we share similar brain structures with mammals. This part of the brain is mainly interested in survival. The subcortical region is where our emotional reactions come from.

The subcortical regions contain an area of the brain known as the limbic system. The limbic system and the area beneath it are where emotions are generated. The amygdala, which is located on both sides of the brain, in particular triggers emotions such as anxiety.

The part of the brain that Big Jim calls 'the minder' is technically known as the prefrontal cortex. The prefrontal cortex is an extremely important part of the brain in terms of human evolution. It acts as a messenger between the neocortex and the primitive brain regions that lie beneath it.

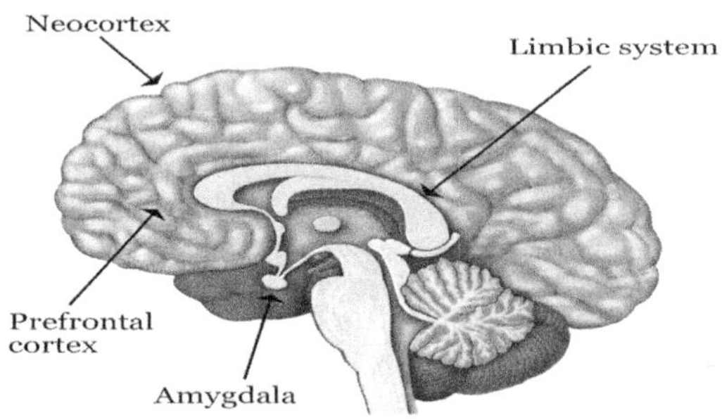

The Brain

Emotions exercise

1. Begin by noticing where you feel your emotion most strongly.
2. Keep your focus on your feeling. Place your hand wherever you feel your emotion more strongly. You are placing your hand on your body where your emotion is, because many of us who are prone to avoiding emotions unconsciously and automatically move away from feeling emotions, and go into our heads instead. You are gaining a connection with your emotions and keeping your focus on how you are feeling. Placing your hand on the part of your body where you feel your anxiety more strongly will also act as a reminder to you to keep your focus on your emotions. It is very important while you are doing this exercise to focus on feeling your feelings and remind yourself that you really are willing for your emotions to be there.
3. Focusing on the part of your body underneath your hand with your mind, examine exactly what your emotion feels like. For example, how much space do your feelings take up? How painful or uncomfortable are your feelings? Rate the intensity of your feeling between 1 and 10, where 10 is the highest level of intensity. While you continue to feel your feelings, mentally give your feelings permission to take up the space that they are taking up in your body. If you want to take things a little further, you could also speak to your distress. Internally, try saying something along the lines of 'Thank you for being there' ... 'There are very good reasons for you being there.' Bear in mind the idea that, from the primitive mind's point of view, there is a good reason for your anxiety being there, even if it does not make sense logically. Follow that by saying 'You are welcome to stay there for as long as you want.'
4. Bear in mind from the subcortical region's (primitive mind's) point of view that if it notices during its screening process that there is a cue to a potential threat, which may be physical or psychological, it is just doing its job properly if it brings the threat to your attention and helps you to prepare. The threat does not need to be logical, real or valid in the current time mode. If it has been perceived as a threat in the past, or you have previously confirmed the existence of the threat by withdrawing from this threat in the past, then from the primitive mind's point of view the threat is still active.
5. While feeling your symptoms of anxiety it is important when you speak to your feelings that you really mean what you are saying. Let go of all your thoughts and focus on your feeling. The importance of your self-communication is not in the words that you use but rather your intention behind your words. Keep an idea in mind of accepting, recognising, being grateful and being patient. Do this for a minute or so and bring your awareness to what happens.
6. Stay with your emotions as the intensity gradually decreases.
7. It is important in the early stages of CBT when you are experiencing anxiety, low mood, guilt and anger to practise being with your feelings as much as possible. This will help you in two ways. First, it will help you to fear your feelings less; second, it will make it more likely that you will be able to use this acceptance approach when you are experiencing higher levels of distress.

8. Bear in mind that in a state of heightened distress the frontal lobes – where most of our logical thinking occurs – stop working somewhat. Doing the same thing over and over again when you are not so distressed will make it more likely that you will be able to access and use this approach automatically when you really need it.

Potential behavioural experiments for OCD

SAFETY BEHAVIOUR	NEW ALTERNATIVE BEHAVIOUR
Avoid situations or people that may trigger intrusive thoughts.	Carry out daily activities. Do not avoid people or places that you come across.
Retrace steps.	Postpone retracing steps.
Go back and check things that you are unsure of.	If you have checked once already, leave it.
Complete ritualistic behaviour, for example, touching wood.	Postpone ritualistic behaviour and wait for urge to die down.
Complete mental calculations in head to distract from emotions.	Put 100% attention onto feeling feelings.
Push away intrusive thoughts if you believe that thinking about them will make them real.	Recognise intrusive thoughts. Allow them to come and go in their own time.
Complete activities a certain number of times.	Reduce the number of times that you complete activities.
Perform activities in a particular order.	Deliberately change the order.
Wear particular make-up or jewellery.	Change make-up or jewellery.
Carry certain items.	Leave items behind for gradually longer periods of time.
Check and re-check that you have not left anything behind.	Check once and go.
Look for reassurance for others.	Drop reassurance.
Encourage others to engage in checks or rituals.	If you need to complete a checking behaviour, do it on your own. Ask relatives not to cooperate with completing obsessional behaviours.
Stay with safe people.	Spend time away from safe people.
Clean things to avoid contamination.	Reduce cleaning activity. Postpone cleaning.
Hold on to items or hoard things.	Gradually throw away things that you don't need any more. Throw away at least one piece of clutter a day.

Glossary

Beliefs: Unconditional thinking patterns that cannot be proved or disproved using evidence.

Cognitive distortions: Biased thinking patterns associated with heightened distress

Formulations: Psychological explanations of presenting problems

Genetic: Occurs naturally as a result of predetermined factors.

Habits: Behaviours that we are inclined to use because we have used them so many times before.

Intrusive thoughts: Thoughts that enter awareness uninvited. These thoughts are usually accompanied by heightened emotion.

Meditation: A process of staying in the present moment, bringing conscious awareness back to the present, and deliberately moving away from thoughts about the past or the future.

Neocortex: Outer layer of the brain responsible for complex thought.

Neutralising behaviours: Behaviours that are used to take away uncomfortable feelings.

Over-inflated sense of responsibility: When an individual takes on too much responsibility for factors that are outside of the individual's control.

Rituals: Behaviours that we carry out in a particular order.

Safety behaviours: Behaviours used to reduce emotional distress in the short term.

Printed in Great Britain
by Amazon

35366539R00086